Performance
Rock Climbing

Dale Goddard and Udo Neumann

STACKPOLE
BOOKS

Published by
STACKPOLE BOOKS
5067 Ritter Road
Mechanicsburg, PA 17055
www.stackpolebooks.com

Printed in the United States of America

10

First Edition

Cover design by Mark Olszewski
Illustrations by Gerold Graw
Photographs by Udo Neumann

Library of Congress Cataloging-in-Publication Data

Goddard, Dale.
    Performance rock climbing / Dale Goddard and Udo Neumann. — 1st ed.
       p.   cm.
    ISBN 0-8117-2219-8
    1. Rock climbing. 2. Rock climbing—Training. I. Neumann, Udo.
II. Title.
GV200.2.G63   1993
796.5'25—dc20   93-16842
                                      CIP

ISBN 978-0-8117-2219-3

An Important Note to Readers

This book contains much useful information about the sport of rock climbing. Before engaging in this potentially hazardous sport however, you must do more than read a book.

The sport requires skill, concentration, physical strength and endurance, proper equipment, knowledge of fundamental principles techniques, and unwavering commitment to your own safety and that of your companions.

The publisher and author obviously cannot be responsible for your safety. Because rock climbing entails the risk of serious and even fatal injury, we emphasize that you should not begin climbing except under expert supervision. No book can substitute for pro training and experience under the guidance and supervision of a qualified teacher.

CONTENTS

ACKNOWLEDGMENTS

Thanks to Mike Beck, Dave Bell and his Body Shop, Cathy Beloeil, Steve Bleyl, Maria Cranor, Robyn Erbesfield, Will Gadd, Dominique Gudmundsdottir, Amy Irvine, Erik Jensen, Jonathon Knight, Karen Peil, Bob Richards and Rockreation, Boone Speed, Jean Baptiste Tribout, Marc Twight, Martin Yoisten, and April Walters for her tolerance throughout our "three month" project.

INTRODUCTION

This book is about improving at rock climbing. It is not a learning-to-climb book like several already on the shelves. We don't discuss knot tying or belay safety. We've written for climbers already versed in the technicalities of equipment use and safety who hope to hone the athletic abilities that climbing demands.

Some will ask, "Why should I want to improve?" and indeed, this is a valid question. After all, the satisfaction of simply "doing" the sport is tremendous. The act of climbing is inherently enjoyable at any level. It takes you to places and situations distinct from those of your everyday life. It puts you in circumstances where you feel your own strength and that of the natural environment. It introduces you to diverse people. You don't need to be trying to climb better to enjoy these aspects of climbing.

But improvement in itself is a source of satisfaction independent of those described above. You sense this when you're working on a difficult sequence and someone suggests a subtle shift in body weight that replaces a grimacing power movement with a graceful one. You see it more clearly on the days when the results of your training show themselves—your climbing "clicks," and you feel smooth and fluid on moves that normally require everything you can muster. You know it in your heart on those rare and precious days when the many skills climbing demands come together at once, weaving preparation and spontaneity together into one unforgettable ascent.

Seeking improvement doesn't detract from the pleasure of doing. Many derive satisfaction from playing the piano for years with the same degree of skill. Yet people agree that with increased ability, the richness and depth of the experience grows. Climbing is no different. The more you put into it, the richer your harvest.

Improvement in climbing is not reserved for the ambitious energy of youth. Climbing is a sport one can pursue safely for the long term, and progress continues as long as there's motivation behind it. In France, parents climb alongside their children at the cliffs, all of them improving with age. And look at Alan Steck, pioneer of early Yosemite classics. Now in his sixties, Steck continues to improve and now leads 5.10. To celebrate his sixtieth birthday, he free-climbed Yosemite's *Steck-Salathé*, which he established as an aid route in the early 1950s.

Pursuing improvement is not without pitfalls, however. There's no guarantee you'll reach your aim. Improvement can come quickly or not at all, depending on how you go about it. Train right and you'll steadily increase your ability; choose the wrong approach and you might actually regress.

In today's world, we all have limits to the amount of time we can dedicate to any pursuit. Some of the activities that enhance rock-climbing skills suspend the immediate rewards of the sport in hope of future payoffs. If you make such an investment, you want to feel sure it will be worthwhile.

Also important is how improvement comes. If you progress rapidly one month, then plateau the rest of the season, you'll feel frustration rather than satisfaction. If hoped-for advancement is sporadic, rewarding you one month then disappointing you the next, you're likely to view your desire to improve as a source of unhappiness. So if climbing is to add something positive to your life, your training must produce consistent improvement and allow you to meet your expectations.

The pitfalls mentioned above occur only to the extent that you lack experience and knowledge about how to improve at climbing. To avoid them you need to deepen your understanding of the skills that contribute to climbing performance. When Udo interviewed the head Soviet climbing coach, Alexander Piratinskij, at the 1991 World Championships, he asked if Piratinskij was surprised at his team's successes in recent competitions. "No," he smiled, as he spread his arms. "We have a broad base of knowledge." By providing such knowledge, this book aims to increase the joy that comes from climbing well.

CAST OF CHARACTERS

Three imaginary characters peered over our shoulders as we wrote this book. As a result we will trail Julia, Bruno, and Max through their successes and failures as they negotiate the obstacles to improving at climbing. We can learn from their mistakes and profit from their insights. Although they're fictional characters, they are modeled after the real people we all know in climbing, and their experiences stem from real-life episodes.

Julia

Julia is a career woman who started climbing a year ago with her boyfriend, Bruno. Julia has practiced many sports in her life: ballet and gymnastics when she was young, then tennis and running later on. During the last four years she's done aerobics a few times weekly, staying in shape despite her sedentary job. Low on arm and shoulder strength, Julia sneaks through climbing cruxes with technique.

She's twenty-six years old, five-foot-seven, and 128 pounds.

Julia

Bruno

Bruno is an ex-marine who has been a weekend climber for twelve years. Although he has little experience in sports, he was a long-time body-builder before reorienting his weight lifting toward climbing a year ago. He has led easy 5.10 for the last three years. His motivations are to be outside,

Bruno

have fun with his pals, and impress Julia with his feats of strength.

Bruno is thirty-three years old, stands five feet eight inches tall, and weighs 180 pounds.

Max

Twenty-one-year-old Max is willing to do anything to become a better climber, or more precisely, to become the best climber in the universe. He has been climbing for nine years. At five-foot-nine and 130 pounds, Max considers himself built for the big numbers, and from the beginning he has climbed with good climbers and trained for the sport. As a part-time student, Max finds plenty of time to work out, climb, and travel. His issues as an advanced climber will be considered in the different chapters to follow.

Max

1. THE WEAKEST LINK PRINCIPLE

So many different factors contribute to your climbing performance. Where do you begin? Finger strength? Fear? Footwork? Flexibility? Methods are known for increasing your ability in most of the individual skills involved in climbing. The problem is just that none of us has the time to work on all of them. We must pick and choose. Spend your time on the wrong one and you might stagnate, as too many climbers do.

The flip side of this complexity is that informed training can produce dramatic progress. But to make such gains, you need an effective overall approach and a way to decide which aspects to work on, which to ignore, and when to change focus.

If you spend too much time with your head buried in a weight-training manual, it's easy to forget that getting stronger is not an end in itself. People get so caught up in the details of how to get stronger or lose weight that goals like these eclipse the original aim, which was to improve their climbing. To illustrate the kinds of traps this leads climbers into, let's try an analogy.

BUILDING A BETTER MACHINE

Imagine that you and your friends decided that for a hobby you would each get an old, sputtering VW bug. You'd work on your respective cars individually, but sometimes you'd congregate and do this work together. You could give each other suggestions about one another's cars if you wanted to, but you could do work only on your own car. By working on it over a period of years, you

hoped to gradually make yourself a high-performance vehicle.

Looking at your shabby car, it's clear that many different types of improvement would help its performance. But since the car's most immediate problem is that it won't go faster than twenty miles an hour and it slows to a near crawl on steep terrain, you decide to work on its engine. By tuning your vehicle's powerhouse, you hope to make higher speeds possible.

You study engine power. You devise refinements that make your engine deliver more power on command. As time goes on, your progress is unmistakable. You don't have a race-car engine, and you could keep improving your engine's performance for years, but nonetheless, you eventually make great strides toward a better engine.

Now your car can attain speeds of forty miles per hour on the flats and can hold twenty mph on steeper grades. In fact, it could probably go even faster except that horrible trembling starting at thirty-five nearly cripples the car at speeds over forty.

On any kind of cornering or complex maneuvers, steering becomes a problem. Loose play in the steering, which had no effect on performance when the engine was weaker, is now the limiting factor in your car's driving. But you're happy with your improvement and have the satisfaction of knowing that your car performs much better now than it did at the start.

What do you work on next? This is where too many people fail in their performance-enhancing strategy. Having become specialists in one aspect of their vehicle's performance, they prefer to continue working on that area, even when their efforts could be focused more productively on other aspects.

Since you have no experience with other cars, you're probably unaware of your own car's strengths and weaknesses—you've never had another car to compare it with. So you're tempted to continue the kind of work you're familiar with and to diagnose your vehicle's shortcomings in terms of your

specialty rather than switching to an area foreign to you. "Of course my vehicle shakes at high speeds," you rationalize. "If I just had more power, I could push through it."

As an engine specialist of sorts, you enjoy working on your engine. After all, you know that part of your car best and you're proud of it. When you're working alongside your friends, you can lift your hood with pride, knowing that the fruits of your months of efforts will be apparent.

Like it or not, there is an unspoken pressure to show some immediate results. No one wants to feel he's been wasting his time, and the best way to receive social strokes for your efforts is to work on the area you've developed best. If you concentrated on your steering while your friends were honing and shining the most impressive parts of their machines, onlookers would certainly conclude that your friends' cars were in much better shape.

So you continue to work on your engine.

Working on his strengths, Bruno can lift his hood with pride, knowing the results of his efforts will show.

After applying yourself for a whole year, you've developed so much engine power that you can force your car through the thirty-five- to forty-mph vibrations and even drive smoothly, until more violent vibrations begin at fifty-five. Of course, you still can't maneuver any better than you could before, but your acceleration is now good enough that you can make up for some lost time on straightaways. Unfortunately, now that you know what it's like to go fast, you'd like to take some longer rides, but your rusty, cracked fuel tank holds only a couple gallons of gas.

You've now reached a critical point in your work on the car. Although you're still far from having a high-performance engine, another whole year's worth of work on your engine will not add anything to the real-life performance of your car. The best engine in the world won't keep your steering from shaking or your limited tank from draining. Although there are still measures by which you could continue to gauge improvements to your engine, your car's performance will remain plateaued until you address its weakest areas. By contrast, a minor tuning of the steering or replacement of the fuel tank would have a dramatic effect on your driving.

THE WEAKEST LINK PRINCIPLE

This leads to what we call the weakest link principle. Your car's performance derives from an elaborate chain of abilities that must act in concert to produce motion. Although performance represents the combined result of many different abilities, it is not the simple sum of them. Performance will be pulled down to the level of the weakest of the abilities you must use in a given situation. Just as a chain is only as strong as its weakest link, your vehicle's performance will be limited by its weakest areas.

A small change in your weakest areas will have a great effect on overall performance, while a significant improvement in the strongest areas will have a much smaller effect. For this reason, maximizing improvement requires discovering your weakest areas and targeting them as your top training priorities.

If you work on any one area long enough, you eventually reach a point at which your efforts would be more profitably applied to weaker aspects of your performance. The challenge, then, is deciding which are your priority areas. Finding your weak spots is a matter of asking yourself the right questions and persistently examining your climbing. Self-examination will shed light on the weak facets of the repertoire of skills you bring to your climbing.

Seeking your weaknesses shouldn't be regarded as "dwelling on the negative." On the contrary, learning about your weaknesses is like discovering a gold mine, for this is where your potential for improvement lies. Self-knowledge is the source of your ability to grow. It's the climber who *doesn't* know his weaknesses whose future is dark, because he has no focus for his efforts. His is the discouraging state, for his gains will be sporadic and random at best.

You need not forget your strengths. They will continue to give you confidence and motivation. But it is through your work on your weaknesses that you improve.

sting was the fact that he had just finished a winter of intensely dedicated training, which had added significantly and measurably to his already vast reservoir of power.

Since power was an area in which Güllich was already rich, gains in this domain had few noticeable effects on his climbing performance. Lack of power was not his limitation before his winter of training, and it wasn't his problem after his season in the gym.

His words revealed not only the frustration of choosing a wrong priority, but also insight into his error. Climbing is a complex summation of many skills, and it was skill areas he had neglected that held him back. Güllich returned home, changed his training focus to weaker areas, and went on to put up the first 13d in the world, *Kanal im Rücken,* seven months later (1984).

Weaknesses Often Wear Masks

Bruno and Julia first met while bouldering. Bruno was proud of the results of his finger and strength training and was eager to show them off on a boulder problem that had haunted him since the preceding season. *The Aggression Roof* was rated 5.10a and took an impressive line out a five-foot overhang.

Hot for the rock, Bruno started up and out the roof. With hands midway out, his feet slipped unexpectedly off the back wall. He stabilized and reassured himself, "Steep climbing is all strength anyway." As if doing another pullup at the gym, Bruno chinned the holds and shot a hand out to the lip. He managed to catch it and steady his helicoptering feet, readying himself for the next and hardest move.

Wolfgang Güllich on Sale Temps.

Different weaknesses lead to different training needs. The following examples illustrate the role of weaknesses and priorities in climbing and the diversity of problem areas that confront climbers.

Working Strengths Does Little for Performance

"Climbing is so complex!" lamented Germany's top climber, the late Wolfgang Güllich, at the point of tears.

It was early in the climbing season, and he'd been trying *Sale Temps* (5.13b) in France's Verdon Gorge for five days without success. What made his failed efforts

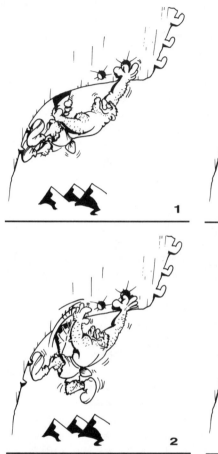

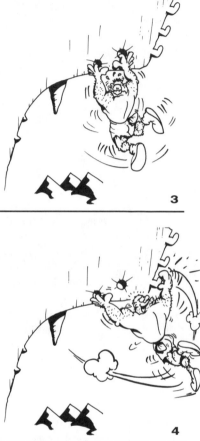

With arms spread wide, he knew he'd swing hard when he went for it. With a powerful pull, he bolted his left hand over the lip, straining to hold on against the gyrating outward tug of his swing.

Bruno's hands were slick with sweat. Chalking up would mean hanging on by one hand, but he couldn't continue without it. Smiling through his grimace, he chalked

a hasty hand. Unable to get his feet onto the roof's lip, Bruno pulled up desperately, shooting a hand to the final hold to catch himself as he fell out.

With reddened face, he pulled onto the boulder's top, taking his first breath in several moments. His expression betrayed the cocky pride he felt. Scrambling down from his hardest-ever boulder, Bruno told

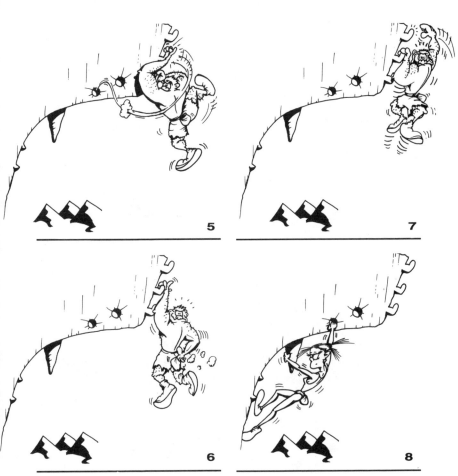

how his diet and strength-training program had shown their results in the last minutes.

With success-inspired generosity, Bruno nodded toward the problem. "Might as well give it a try," he offered to Julia. He smiled to himself in sympathy, certain that success was unlikely. In Bruno's mind, climbing ability depended only on strength. And strength was one thing he knew Julia lacked.

But Julia took a different tack on the roof. By using the rock's features to position her body, she made the moves with her feet on the rock and avoided the swings that were nearly Bruno's downfall. Where Bruno had climbed using a series of lock-offs, Julia kept her arms straight, rolling on her shoulders and pushing herself to within reach of the holds with her feet. At the lip, underclinging

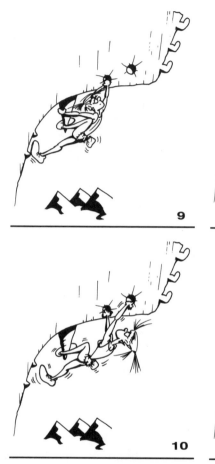

9

11

10

12

the spike with her feet so improved her angle of pull on the handhold that she was able to chalk up casually. Just above, flexibility allowed her to use her feet for the final moves, which she again made straight-armed.

As she rounded the top of the boulder, pumped but still graceful, Bruno stammered, "How can this be?" and was quiet the rest of the day.

Summary of the Weakest Link Principle

- Your weaknesses pull down your climbing performance much more than your strengths buoy it.
- To the extent that our native abilities vary, each of us has different priorities.

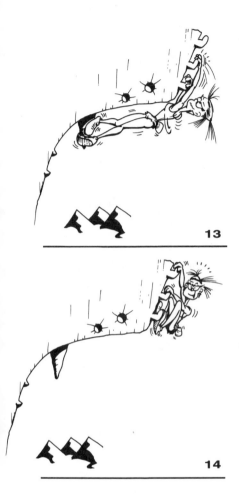

13

14

- Failure to address your ever-changing weak spots leads to plateaus.

Implications of the Weakest Link Principle

The most efficient approach to training for improvement comes from this fundamental principle of the weakest link. Because of this, the approach and philosophy behind effec-

tive training is the same whether you are a World Cup climber or a first-time beginner.

In sports that involve repeating the same moves over and over (running and biking, for instance), fewer abilities contribute to performance, and choosing which to work on is easier. The breadth of abilities involved in climbing makes this choice more difficult but also makes climbing unique among sports.

Identifying, learning about, and monitoring your priority areas constitute half the battle in training. Because the abilities that affect climbing are diverse, you simply don't have time to work on all of them at once. What's more, it is sometimes difficult to know your strengths and weaknesses, because you haven't lived with any others. Choosing the wrong priority sabotages your progress. Rapid improvement can come only when you focus your attention on two or three genuine priorities.

Many climbers assume that the best way to train must be to copy whatever the best climbers are doing. After all, these climbers have tried many different approaches and have presumably chosen the methods that produce the greatest results. But because weaknesses vary with individuals as much as personalities do, the specifics of an effective training program necessarily vary greatly from climber to climber. The optimal way for one climber to spend his time is useless for another climber of the same ability whose weaknesses differ.

Improving as a climber compares with any project of craftsmanship: desire, ambition, and hard work will be wasted if they are not directed intelligently. The drawback of climbing's complexity is that one must be ever mindful to continue progressing. But when mastery at any level occurs, the rewards of climbing tower over the satisfactions other sports have to offer.

CLIMBING AS A MULTIFACETED SPORT

Climbing is a sport of complexity and contrasts. Using strength tempered by technique, trying to ensure safety in an environment of potential danger, and balancing precariously between anxiety and determination, the climber finds pathways through the impossible.

Climbing performance is an expression of the whole person and must be regarded as a summation of many different conditions and abilities. The factors that affect climbing performance fall into the six categories described in the diagram below.

The boundaries between these categories intermingle, and the different categories influence each other. For example, motivation affects physical strength; protection affects fear; fear affects coordination; flexibility affects technique; and body height affects tactics.

In this book we will examine all the aspects of a climber's performance that are open to change. With each of the major topics, a chapter of background information is followed by one or two chapters dedicated to more concrete training techniques, in which we show how to apply this information to improve your climbing.

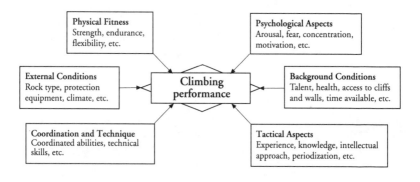

2. COORDINATION

On good days, climbers report, "It just happened. I didn't really think a lot while I was doing it. It just came naturally." The body makes clean, crisp moves in the ways the rock demands, and it's not a battle. You climb with technique.

On bad days, climbing often feels like your thinking mind is working excessively and your technique is out to lunch. Paralyzing consideration replaces instinctive action. Climbing routes pit your physical resources against gravity. As a result, climbing requires strength, endurance, and flexibility. A given quantity of these physical resources, however, doesn't correspond directly to a particular level of skill at the cliffs. Some climbers use their physical resources wisely, expending the minimum necessary to accomplish the moves before them. Others use them unwisely, squandering twice as much energy as the situation requires.

Physical assets like power and endurance aren't the only factors that influence performance. Your use of these physical resources is controlled by how well you move your body—by the sports-specific movement skills we call technique.

What defines good technique?

The answer is efficiency.

Unfortunately, we aren't objective judges of our own efficiency. We're practiced at some techniques and bad at others. Sometimes it's hard to believe that techniques we're bad at are even worth learning. When we're weak at an efficient technique, it can feel harder than a less efficient technique

we're practiced at. Consider the muscular climber who has poor foot technique. When others suggest that Bruno improve his footwork, he scoffs, saying, "Why should I work on footwork? When I take time to place my feet carefully and use 'technique,' my arms fatigue faster than if I just power through the difficult section."

It's true. Bruno really is less efficient when he's concentrating on footwork, but not because using careful footwork is less efficient than thugging it. Bruno's not accustomed to using his feet. As a result, it takes all his concentration every time he tries to do so. And with his focus stolen away for footwork, he slows down, tightens up, and tires out. The lesson is simple: you can't judge the relative effectiveness of a technique or style of climbing until you have actually developed some ability in that technique.

How do you develop it? Let's look at where technique comes from. Technique derives from your body's control of physical movement—from your coordination abilities. This chapter addresses the nature of physical coordination as background for two chapters on technique training. This basic understanding is prerequisite to constructive technique training. If you skip the background and simply learn the training methods, you're likely to make errors in applying them.

Learn about coordination and you'll have a powerful tool for developing your technique. Apply it smartly and you'll transform your climbing.

Muscle Spindles

Muscle spindles are sensory receptors within muscles. They compare the length of a "test fiber" within the muscle to that of a normal muscle fiber. They are useful in several ways.

First, spindles provide the reflexes that stabilize body positions against outside forces. When a muscle is stretched against your will, the spindle is lengthened and its receptors report this length change to your brain. This allows contraction to be adjusted to prevent or slow further lengthening.

For example, imagine someone tosses you a water bottle with an unknown amount of water in it. The spindles allow you to adjust the contractions in your arms as you catch it so that you compensate with just enough force to bring it to rest, neither dropping it nor jerking it upward.

Second, spindles protect the body against harm. A sudden lengthening of a muscle's spindles causes the muscle to contract. The *stretch reflex* prevents muscle damage that could occur when muscles are pulled too rapidly or stretched too far.

FOUNDATIONS OF COORDINATION

Consider something we're all familiar with: riding a bicycle. When a child is learning to ride, every aspect of the process engages him mentally, and his movements are rough and jerky. When the bicycle tips and the child compensates with a shift in the handlebars, he teeters, quivers, and sometimes falls. While riding, the wobbling child is so mentally involved in just staying balanced that he can barely spare any attention for where he is going or what's happening around him.

After two weeks, however, an incredible change has occurred. The movements are wired and no longer require overpowering mental focus. The child's consciousness is completely free, and he not only rides smoothly and steadily, he negotiates obstacles, plans for upcoming terrain, or even converses while riding. The same task that formerly demanded full mental focus he now performs with plenty of awareness to spare.

As climbers, we too start out with difficulty moving and an almost overwhelming mental engagement. We spend more time hesitating between jerky moves than we do actually climbing. But transformations like the bicyclist's occur for climbers too. They allow us not only to move more efficiently but also to have more free awareness for planning and strategy on a pitch. To understand how such changes occur, we must look at the hidden operators responsible for them: *motor engrams.* [1]

[1] The term engram has been adopted by the Church of Scientology to describe psychological phenomena. We use the term in its biological sense and emphasize that it bears no connection to Scientology's use.

Controlling Movement

At every instant, whether we are moving or not, our brains receive sensory feedback from our limbs. These signals come from nerves in our muscles, tendons, joints, and skin. They tell the brain about muscle contractions, body positions, and forces acting on us.

This constant stream of kinesthetic information is the source of our body awareness. The information it conveys, especially that from muscle spindles (see box on page 14), allows the brain to oversee and control movement.

Governing any movement involving the whole body is an extremely complex process. Each of our 425 skeletal muscles needs constantly adjusted instructions from the brain. In first-time-ever movements, the brain does this by monitoring kinesthetic signals, analyzing them, and feeding responses back to the muscles. Because of the amount of information exchange involved, this process pushes the motor area of the brain to its limit. As a result, first-time movements are often stiff and jerky, and the mind feels fully absorbed by the task. Fortunately, the brain learns from experience and has alternatives in controlling movement.

Engrams Record and Replay

When a climber executes a movement, the motion causes a particular sequence of nerve impulses, unique to that specific movement, to occur in the brain. When he repeats the movement several times (whether in reality or through accurate mental imagery), the repetition of that pattern of nerve impulses ingrains the movement in memory and causes it to be stored as a motor engram. (From here on we'll refer to motor engrams simply as engrams.")

Engrams are complete records of movements we've made. More important, they're also the instruction manuals for reproducing the same movements at will. Engrams contain all the directions necessary to reproduce living versions of moves stored in memory. You could think of an engram as a packet of preset muscle instructions on how to reproduce a particular move.

Since it can replace thousands of conscious signals, using an engram to control a movement makes it unnecessary for the brain to constantly monitor all of the kinesthetic feedback and send out corrected signals. This frees the brain to work on other issues and makes more complex movements possible.

For example, many dynamic climbing moves require a precise sequential involvement of different muscle groups. Thrust too early with your feet and you won't push in the right direction; thrust too late and the holds will be out of range. In such cases, there's no time for the brain to monitor and give feedback in midcourse. As a result, such moves can be impossible to do until your body has "learned" an engram for the move and can do it without thinking along the way.

A climbing route or boulder problem therefore feels much easier after you have done it several times. Each repetition strengthens the engram for that sequence of moves, reducing the conscious monitoring necessary. After extensive practice your body "knows" how to do it. This is why peak performances are characterized by a quiet mind and a sensation that things are accomplished "without thinking about it." Research confirms that the brain is most active while learning a new skill. Once proficient, it does a better job with less work using engram control.

Engrams' effectiveness at reproducing the moves they record depends on how recently and how frequently they have been used. The more use an engram receives, the better it reproduces its pattern into real movement. The longer it has been since its last use, the rustier it will be.

The Inner Theater

Shifting to engram control is not a conscious process. Instead, the brain compares kinesthetic information it takes in while climbing to the patterns stored in its engrams. It searches for an engram that matches the situation at hand. If it finds a match, then engram control is an option.

The brain uses an "inner theater" to solve a given climbing problem before executing the move in real life. When faced with a crux move, your brain searches for an engram to fit the arrangement of holds before you. Looking at the holds, your brain might see three different sequence possibilities. Playing them on its inner stage, it compares their kinesthetic "feel" to those of engrams stored in memory. If the sequences are significantly different from the moves stored as engrams, monitoring and constantly adjusted feedback must govern the move. If a stored engram feels right, it can direct the movement, reducing the need for mental monitoring.

With ready access to a large repertoire of engrams, the inner theater can prevent errors before they are made.

Consider Max as he starts up a route he has top-roped several times before. As he climbs, his brain compares the holds before him and the moves they require to holds and moves stored in his engrams. On recognizing familiar moves, his brain initiates the engrams he has formed for them. Because he has climbed the route many times, his engrams for these moves are strong and his movements are smooth, deliberate, and efficient.

As long as the route's moves match those in Max's memory, engram control dominates. Although adjustments to the engrams might be necessary ("sweatier skin today, hold on tighter"), Max's body runs predominantly on autopilot, and his mind has time for activities like pacing himself and thinking of strategies to conserve strength.

When Max moves over to a route he hasn't been on before, his brain no longer finds matches between the moves he must make and those stored in his engram memory. Since the situation at hand doesn't fit his existing engrams, the slow-going monitoring/feedback process dominates Max's climbing. As for a beginner on a bike, each shift in weight is new to him and begs at his awareness for attention. Consequently, Max is focused on each movement he makes and can spare less thought for upcoming sections or overall tactics.

Sometimes on this pitch, however, Max comes upon a move resembling one from other routes he knows well. On recognizing such a move, his movement centers use an engram for it and he climbs it on engram control.

Building a Repertoire

Few sports demand the variety and precision

of movements that climbing does. Running, biking, and rowing all involve the repetition of comparatively few movements. Many sports involving more varied movement don't hinge on their precise execution. In such sports, movement training is not of central importance.

In climbing, the summed effect of tiny movement mistakes or inefficiencies adds up fast. The best climber is not necessarily stronger than the rest—he's the one who makes the fewest movement errors. It's the choice of moves and positions and the speed with which they're chosen that separate climbers.

It nearly always feels like you fall off because your fingers open or you can't hold the hold. Leaving it at that, however, misses the essence of climbing. Whether you fingers open or not depends on *how* you move and how *efficiently* you've gotten to where you are on a route. Climbing is a movement-centered sport.

Like climbing, karate is a sport in which the number of possible moves is nearly unlimited and strength and precision are critical. Climbers should note that practitioners of karate emphasize practicing movement over strength training. In neither sport can one go far by using strength without technique. And in both, a weaker participant with good technique can outperform a much stronger one.

You can climb nearest to your physical potential when you have the moves down pat. Even when climbing a route for the first time, a vast library of engrams allows you to recognize the moves that a particular arrangement of holds requires. When proficient on-sight climbers look at a set of holds, their bodies know instantly what to do with them. This skill requires a lot of experience because of the nearly infinite variety of possible moves. The size of holds, their arrangement and facing directions, their texture and friction, and the angle and shape of the wall they're on all vary. Even slight differences in these factors affect the body position that makes best use of them.

Dealing with these variables efficiently requires a vast reservoir of engrams derived from experiences in comparable situations. The bigger your storehouse of engrams, the more likely you are to find one to match the situations you encounter on a route. Your engram repertoire determines the problem-solving ability of your inner theater.

No climber has become good on-sight without developing a broad repertoire of moves. As a result, the average age of successful on-sight climbers is high compared with that of top athletes in other sports. (The few young on-sight experts are typically mature as athletes and started at an early age.) Success at difficult redpoints doesn't require as much experience; it reflects the ability to perfect specific movements rather than the depth of an engram repertoire.

The engram repertoire explains why climbers rarely skip more than a letter grade in their on-sight development. One hears young, ambitious climbers complaining (in so many words), "I'm tired of working my way through the grades. I wanna flash 5.13 *now!*" To pretend that grades can be skipped denies the role of engram repertoires.

The importance of a vast storehouse of engrams has parallels in other pursuits. World-class chess players spend most of their "training" time learning combinations and positions played at international tournaments. This helps them respond instantly to combinations they recognize before them.

Other Influences on Coordination

Psychological Aspects and Engram Control

Although the mechanisms described above govern movement, other factors can come into play. Specifically, psychological arousal affects your ability to use your engrams.

Under conditions of stress and arousal, we lose access to all but our most ingrained engrams. We revert to earlier levels of ability when we're nervous, and we sometimes lose coordination when people are watching us.

When the monitor/feedback control of movement jumps in too often, it suggests two possibilities: either you lack engrams for the types of moves you face, or your engrams are failing you due to conditions of stress.

In the first case, you must simply do your homework and practice the techniques you lack to broaden your engram repertoire. In the second, the solution lies either in stress-proofing the engrams you have (see the Technique Training chapters) or in learning to lower your arousal level (see the Psychology chapters).

Techniques such as relaxation and visualization, which we'll discuss later, can help to curb excessive conscious involvement in climbing movement when your engrams are strong enough to trust. Once you've acquired a repertoire of moves, on-sighting is about letting go. To use your engrams most effectively, you must get out of your mind and let instinct guide you. Even when moves don't come to you, you solve them best and return to engram reliance fastest when you're in a relaxed, calm, and trusting state of mind.

Lactic Acid

Lactic acid also affects coordination. Although endurance athletes achieve concentrations as high as 20 millimoles per liter of lactic acid in their blood during events, lactic acid begins to impair coordination at just 6 mmol/liter. As a result, climbers rarely achieve levels significantly above this.

In activities that don't require technical precision (like running), lactic acid levels don't limit performance until they're sky-high. But for sports like figure skating and climbing, a small loss of sensitive balance, aim, or accuracy can cripple performance. We all experience this loss of coordination when we're pumped. We become clumsy in our movements and fumble with simple tasks.

Keeping this in mind can help you distinguish between shortcomings that are due to engram weaknesses and those that result from lactic acid buildup in the blood. We'll discuss reducing lactic acid accumulation in the Strength chapters.

CONCLUSIONS

What does all this mean for your training? The physiology behind movement suggests that if you want to improve your technique on rock, you should aim to develop a large inventory of solid engrams. The following chapters on technique training will explore how to do just that.

Climbing is a movement-dependent sport. The vast majority of climbers overlook this fact, preferring to concentrate on more concrete and measurable issues like strength and flexibility. Don't be one of these climbers. No other factors in training rightfully deserve more attention than coordination and technique.

On the surface, climbing can seem like a power struggle pitting you against the rock. But more important than the balance of power is the power of balance. If you increase your endurance by 20 percent, you might climb 20 percent higher up a strenuous route. But learn how to conserve your strength, how to move more efficiently, and how to minimize your energy expenditure through effective technique, and you'll climb things you couldn't touch before.

Cathy Beloeil on Hell.

For most climbers, technique training is the most potent springboard to improvement.

Nothing proves this more convincingly than the fact that with exceptional technique, weak climbers can get up powerful routes. Cathy Beloeil, for instance, redpointed American Fork's powerful 5.13a *Hell* near Salt Lake City, Utah. Despite a series of forceful reaches and robust lock-offs, "It's all technique," Cathy insists. By rolling her shoulders, climbing with straight arms, twisting her lock-offs, and dropping a knee here and there, Cathy snaked her way through moves that defeat climbers with twice her strength. This shows that strength doesn't deserve the undivided attention most climbers give it. (It's also an example of how one's strengths and weaknesses skew one's perception of a route's challenges.)

An effective approach to technique training comes from an understanding of human coordination. Having discussed in the previous chapter how coordination points to the vital role of a broad repertoire of movement engrams in climbing, we can now explore what this means in practical terms. Specifically, we must look at ways of acquiring and accessing such a repertoire for use in climbing.

There are innumerable ways to work on your technique, depending on the specific skill you're training for. Many will be explored in the "hands-on" chapter that follows. But at a deeper level, all technique training relies on fundamental principles that apply regardless of the particular exercise or method you're using. So before we leave the classroom and hit the rocks with exercises to improve your technique, let's look at some principles on which all technique training relies.

FUNDAMENTAL PRINCIPLES

The essence of technique training is engram development. Considering the physiology of movement, the process of adding usable engrams to your repertoire breaks down into two fundamental stages, each with distinct training approaches. The first stage involves acquiring engrams; the second, practicing them. The two stages don't follow each other in simple sequence. A climber may do periods of both during a single climbing day.

Stage One: Acquiring Engrams

The process of acquiring engrams involves learning new movements or developing proficiency at moves in which you have only minimal ability. In practice, it is an experimental way of climbing, where goals of ticking a route or getting to the top of something are suspended in favor of experimentation and movement play. Climbing walls and bouldering are the ideal mediums for this activity, since they make it easy to repeat a particular move several times. The goal of this stage is to improve your ability to execute a move under ideal conditions.

Since your brain is always recording the movements you make and most easily recreates the movements most frequently done in the past, this stage aims to feed your brain only those patterns you want it to reproduce. Repeatedly practicing a move with bad technique only increases your tendency to do it badly in the future. You never erase engram memories of moves you've done poorly. But you can strengthen engrams for well-executed moves through practice.

Since doing a move well is what leads to good execution in the future, steps must be taken to maximize good technique when attempting new movements. Likewise, it's important to minimize poor technique, even when you're learning types of moves you haven't done before.

Learn Technique Fresh

To foster this, engram building should not be done in a state of fatigue. As discussed in the Coordination chapter, fatigue undermines coordination. When muscles work hard, they fill with lactic acid. This tightens muscle fibers in the region and reduces coordination in the brain, disrupting movement fluidity throughout the body. Even worse, neurotransmitter fatigue at the junctions between nerve cells interferes with the commands you send to your muscles.

Does this mean you should never climb fatigued? Of course not, for fatiguing muscles is crucial to strengthening them. It means that once tired, you shouldn't try to acquire or develop *new* techniques. In fact, you should take steps not to damage your technique by staying off moves where your technique is shaky when you're extremely fatigued.

Learn Technique in a Safe Environment

Reward and punishment affect any kind of learning. If Julia hurts herself because she attempts her first long dyno on a high

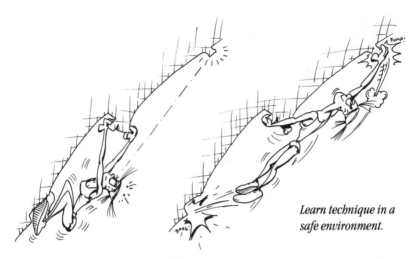

Learn technique in a safe environment.

boulder problem, she'll learn a lot more about injuries than about dynos. But even worse, she'll learn to withdraw from new situations instead of delving into them.

If she works her first dyno close to the ground, on top-rope or next to safe protection, she can fail without punishment. In this situation the reward, when she sticks the dyno, far outweighs the punishment of failed attempts.

Later, once patterns are established, she can transfer these new skills to more challenging situations.

Don't Try to Learn Technique Scared

Fear inhibits athletic performance. In climbing, fear keeps you from trying moves that are near your limits.

But acquiring engrams necessarily involves doing moves that feel uncomfortable and beyond your limit. So feeling safe while experimenting with new technique is doubly important.

Inhibition isn't all bad—it often protects you from danger. But by keeping you far from your limits, it also squelches learning.

The importance of feeling secure while learning new moves partly explains why today's climbers progress so much faster than those of ten years ago. The growing abundance of safe routes has vastly improved the opportunities for learning technique.

Stage Two: Practicing Engrams

Under situations of stress, only your most practiced and instinctive movement engrams are available for your use. So drastic is the tendency for stress, pressure, or risk to cripple all but the most ingrained patterns that Soviet coaches don't consider a trick in a gymnastic routine to be "competition-proof" until the athlete has done it one thousand times.

In the second stage of developing a movement repertoire, you practice the motor engrams you've acquired. You aim to strengthen engrams already in your possession so that they are accessible to you under the more stressful conditions encountered on climbs.

Climbers experience the crippling effects of stress early in their development. "If that move had been next to the ground, I would have cruised it. But something inside held me back, and I climbed like a beginner again." The same move that feels casual when you're fresh and confident can seem impossible when you're eighty feet off the ground, five feet over your last protection, and pumped. It's not that you lack the strength or the engram for the move. Indeed you *would* do it if it were just off the ground—but under stress your body reverts to the patterns it's most sure of.

Movement patterns are like habits: your most practiced ones are the easiest to fall back into, whether they're the best ones or not. Since movements come from motor engrams, the way to replace an undesired movement pattern with a new one is to rehearse the new one until it's second nature.

Practice makes good engrams stress-proof, rendering the technique you have mastered in ideal conditions more transferable to the conditions climbers find themselves in when attempting routes. This second stage of developing engrams aims to reduce your tendency to do the following:

- Lose technique as you fatigue
- Lose fluidity under pressure
- Regress in exposed or intimidating terrain

- Become less effective in dangerous situations.

When climbers only do routes at or above their limits, they have little chance to practice successfully incorporating new techniques. When you're at your limit, there's little margin for error or experimentation; unless your engrams for a particular technique are solid, it's difficult to bring it into your climbing.

Practicing technique is most effective when done through a process of *progressive repetition*. Starting out easily, you repeat a particular technique over and over, gradually increasing the stress or fatigue you're under when using it. By starting at a comfortable level, you make it possible to use techniques you're not solid with. By increasing the difficulty of the situations gradually, you practice *success* as you develop. Tailor the difficulty to whatever it takes for you to succeed at the technique as your proficiency grows.

Let's consider ways of using progressive repetition for the different types of stress climbers encounter.

Fatigue

Imagine that in climbing a friend's boulder problem in the gym, you've just done your first real deadpoint. To use progressive repetition to practice the move, you repeat it over and over in ever greater states of fatigue. You may start by simply doing the same problem later in your workout each time you climb. With each session, you'll know it better but have less power left when you get to it. Next, you could add moves to the start of the problem, or traverse into it so that you're more fatigued when you get to the deadpoint move.

Ideally, you "up the ante" gradually enough that you are successful at the deadpoint most of the time. But push it hard enough that you fail once in a while, just to confirm where your limitations lie. Through this process, you gain comfort with new techniques at the fastest possible rate.

Doing laps on a route by climbing the route, lowering to the ground, and repeating the process on top-rope is another form of progressive repetition. If it's the right difficulty, on each successive effort you know the moves better but are more fatigued. As fatigue and efficiency at the moves increase together, the stress-proofing effect of progressive repetition occurs.

Too often, success marks the end of a climber's attempts on a boulder problem or route. Given what we know about learning technique, being able to do a move or sequence should mark only the beginning of the process of really making it yours through progressive repetition.

Competitive Pressure

Quiet, isolated training days in the sun may do little to prepare you for the pressures of climbing in either informal or organized competitive situations. Climbers whose technique suffers amidst competition or before audiences need to practice using their techniques at progressively increasing levels of the same kind of pressure.

For example, the pressure of having one important chance on a route can be simulated by friendly wagers, mock competitions, or bets about who can do a problem first or how many tries it will take.

Discomfort at climbing in front of people won't go away by avoiding it. If it's a problem you want to solve, bite your lip and put yourself in ever more "public" climbing situations.

Intimidating Situations

Many climbers lose their technique any time they fear falling. You learn to keep hold of your technique in such circumstances by making a conscious effort to climb technically well in progressively more difficult or more intimidating situations.

To do this, make technique your priority for a few weeks. Start by climbing on routes easy enough that you can devote your attention to moving well. Then gradually raise the difficulty or intimidation of subsequent routes. If you revert to poor technique on a route, lower the difficulty or intimidation of the next one. This progressive approach will help you to climb fluidly and effectively right up to your limit.

Remember, failing on a route or choosing the wrong solution to a crux doesn't mean you weren't climbing with good technique. It's only when you fail to climb up to the technical standard *you* know you are capable of that your technique has been compromised by the stress of the situation; when this happens you need to step back in your progression of stress-proofing.

Using progressive desensitization (see Behavioral Approaches to Psychological Control) can also help to habituate you to intimidating situations and reduce their negative impact on your technique.

Dangerous Situations

Some climbers find pleasure in confronting dangerous situations and overcoming them. Since the consequences of failing at this aspect of climbing are serious, care must be taken not to exceed your limits.

Practicing movement engrams in any of these situations will increase your ability to use them under similar adverse conditions. Just remember the rule of training specificity. The best transfer from training to performance will occur when your training most closely simulates the conditions you're training for.

Combining the Two Stages of Engram Learning

Although you can't practice motor engrams until you have acquired them, the practicing stage doesn't mark the end of the learning stage in a climber's progression. A beginner will spend more time acquiring new movement engrams and an expert more time practicing, but learning good technique is an ongoing process of acquiring new engrams and practicing them into solidity. No climber has a 100-percent complete repertoire of movements.

As strength and technical expertise increase, so does the range of possible movements the body can make. As you progress, more techniques become possible for you physically. Thus each significant increment of progress makes possible a return to the learning phase of technique.

The needs of the two stages of technical training affect its ideal scheduling in a day of climbing or training. Since acquiring engrams is best done when you are fresh, it should be worked on early in the day. This stage combines well with bouldering, because both power and engram learning

benefit from being fresh and taking rests between attempts.

Since stress-proofing your technique through progressive repetition requires subjecting your established techniques to progressively less ideal conditions, it is best scheduled later in a climbing day or training session as fatigue sets in, or on the last of consecutive days before a rest day.

Many climbers don't consider their day complete until they have failed on several routes. They regard failure as the only sufficient proof of muscular fatigue to justify stopping for the day. While muscular fatigue is a valid goal for strength development, repeated failure conflicts with the goals of technique training.

Fortunately, strength results can be achieved without compromising technical progress. The rule is to simply take steps to ensure success on moves even as you fatigue. In choosing routes for a workout, select a difficulty that allows you to flirt with muscular failure without falling off. As your fatigue increases, choose routes that are less and less technical. This spares your technique by preventing you from solidifying bad engrams, and it improves strength training by assuring that you fall off only when you reach physical (and not technical) failure.

Avoiding bad technique is important for everyone, but it's especially critical for beginners who are laying down the foundations of their technique. Beginners know few techniques well enough to execute them well when tired, so they must be especially careful not to ingrain bad technique as they fatigue. This doesn't mean they can't train strength on rock, but simply that they should train strength only on routes they know they can do or have done in the past.

There's a popular myth that to improve you must hold your body at the point of physical failure throughout your training, and constantly push "beyond your limits" in all aspects of training. This myth has been bolstered by sensationalized reports of the unending training days of the successful "Euros." But the folly of making this a general approach should be obvious. It implies spending all your time using the relatively few techniques that come to you when you're stressed. It allows no time for acquiring new techniques and practicing them to the point where they're comfortable for you in that state.

Always pushing to the point of physical failure may be appropriate at certain times of the year, for climbers who already have a fairly large repertoire of efficient techniques. Climbing at your limit does help you stress-proof techniques you're already proficient at. But making that your standard procedure misses the whole point. If you haven't developed good and broad technique, there's no point in stress-proofing it. You can't replace bad habits with new techniques if you're always at your limit.

If you want to develop new and better techniques, you have to first spend time experimenting, practicing, and ingraining them, none of which is possible when you're climbing at your limit. Doing this effectively necessitates acquiring the basic movement patterns—motor engrams—in a fresh state, then repeating and practicing them on easy to moderate terrain. Once again, your training must reflect your personal needs.

ISSUES IN TECHNIQUE TRAINING

By Yourself or with a Partner?

Technique flourishes under scrutiny. It takes careful observation to notice movement errors and figure out corrections.

Doing this on your own is hard. Mistakes hide themselves behind layers of habit. In addition, climbers can't see their own bodies, so they often mistakenly assume that they're doing a move comparably to someone else. It's almost impossible to kinesthetically imagine movement that differs drastically from any move you have done. Therefore, while it's possible to make progress training technique alone, the lack of external feedback inevitably leads you to dead ends from which it's difficult to escape by yourself.

In other coordination-dependent activities, such as figure skating and gymnastics, athletes are supervised by a trainer who studies their performance. In the former East Germany, computer-assisted interactive video feedback was common. Paddling kayakers were filmed from several angles, and their video image was compared by computer to an "ideal" movement sequence. If the paddler's arms dropped to a less efficient position due to fatigue, an alarm would sound. Through this form of biofeedback the paddler learned to monitor himself.

Although climbing motions are too diverse for such a system, the same results can be reached with a trainer or experienced partner. In bouldering this often occurs naturally as a group of climbers working on the same boulder problem probe its secrets. Climbers watch each other to look for tips about the best sequence or body position on a route. Though competition may exist between partners, the mutual benefits gained from cooperation are usually enough for people to set egos aside. With this in mind, let's look at how partners can help each other become better climbers.

It's satisfying to work with a partner. You not only get feedback on your climbing, you also become better at analyzing others' techniques and thus at spotting your own technical strengths and flaws.

Effective partnerships are between equally good climbers with dissimilar styles. Comparable ability allows you to work on the same routes or boulder problems, while dissimilar styles give you the most to gain from each other. Watching other, preferably better, climbers is also a plus.

The essential ability in working with a partner is learning to spot movement errors, judge their importance, and make your partner (or yourself) aware of them. The following are the basic elements coaches watch for in athletic performance:

- *Accuracy of movement.* Do the climber's hands and feet take holds precisely, or do they fumble before finding their position on a hold?
- *Reliability of movement.* What percentage of attempts are successful?
- *Speed.* Does the climber take a long time to make a move or moves? Does he rush through them without being careful to conserve energy?
- *Reaction time.* This refers to the interval between receiving new information and reacting to it. Can

the climber change plans quickly if a hold is not as expected? Can he make "saves" when a foot or hand slips?

- *Quality of the movement.* Where was the center of gravity? What path did it take during the movement? Was the direction of movement straight or curved? Where was the movement initiated? Was the whole body involved in the movement, or just a part?
- *Use of the body.* What orientations of force do the available holds require? How was the body used to apply these? Are there more biomechanically advantageous ways of doing this? How was the weight distributed between the holds used? Are there ways of using less energy?
- *Effective training.* Is the partner following principles of smart training?

In the answers to these questions lie the secrets of good technique. When you finish trying a move, ask them of yourself or your partner quickly, before drinking, untying tight shoes, or performing a fit of rage for your friends. Figure out what you did right and wrong, and mentally practice it while the sensory traces of the movement are still fresh in your mind. For thirty to sixty seconds after trying a move, your kinesthetic memory of what happened is still vivid, and feedback is most valuable during these moments.

Video Feedback

Video review of your climbing is an excellent tool for correcting discrepancies between your memory and reality and for honing mental training skills. The best benefits to motor learning are achieved when athletes view themselves as soon as possible after their performance. When reviewed within a minute of finishing, your sensory traces are still fresh, and you can most closely associate what you see in the video with your movement memories.

Cross-training

Cross-training uses other sports or activities as a way of improving your chosen sport. If done only for diversion, cross-training will do little more than keep you mediocre in several sports at once. But with care, you can use other sports to improve your climbing. The key is pinpointing your needs, then choosing other sports that target them.

For example, muscles maintain a certain degree of tension even when relaxed. The degree of this natural muscle tension varies from person to person. Those with excessive muscle tension often shake or tremble when climbing. For such climbers, swimming would be preferred over running as a regeneration/recovery exercise (see chapters 11 and 12) because it lowers overall muscle tension.

If spatial or kinesthetic awareness is a weak area, an activity like martial arts or dance can allow you to train the same skills on nonclimbing days or after climbing, when you're too fatigued to effectively train them through climbing. For balance, skateboarding, skiing, and surfing can have a positive transfer to climbing.

If you have problems relaxing while climbing, consider using the techniques described in the chapter on Behavioral Approaches to Psychological Control.

If coordination is a weak area for you, the benefit of a carefully chosen cross-training activity will far outweigh another weight workout in the gym or another day of climbing when your body needs a rest.

The Reminiscence Effect

A phenomenon termed reminiscence has special relevance for technique-dependent activities like climbing. It refers to an improvement in technical abilities due to a period of *inactivity* in the task. This time-off period can range from a month to several years.

Examples of this abound throughout the sporting world, but cases in our sport impress us most as climbers. In 1984, Jerry Moffat was the world's best rock climber. His list of on-sights and redpoints around the world was unmatched. After getting serious tendinitis in 1985, Jerry was forced out of climbing. While he was out, other climbers caught up to and surpassed his standards. With the rest of the world advancing while Jerry rode his motorcycle, no one thought he would do hard routes again, let alone push world standards.

Yet just weeks after a two-year absence from the sport, Jerry was climbing significantly harder than he ever had. With his redpointing of *La Rage de Vivre* (5.14a) in Buoux, France, he seemed to have improved during his layoff. A month later, at a time when few climbers in the world had climbed a single 5.14, Jerry climbed all three of Buoux's 5.14s in a week.

Why should this occur? Research attributes the reminiscence effect to suppressed performance prior to the layoff. The theory focuses on the restructuring of neural command loops. Movement engrams are loops of neural commands that sequentially activate different parts of your brain to make a particular movement happen. A simplified example of a command loop for a single dynamic bouldering move might be "Sag low in preparation, pull in with the arms; press out lower leg; begin reach with left arm; extend upper leg; reach for hold with left hand; control swing with right arm." (In reality, each of these steps would involve thousands of individual muscular commands.)

As new command loops are acquired, unnecessary commands get built in by careless practice and the conditions of learning. "Clench teeth," "hold breath," and "brace for a fall" are some of the more obvious examples in our climbing, but they can also include extra body movements and unnecessary contractions of noninvolved muscles. When there's no significant break in the practice of the activity, the brain is incapable of ridding itself of these unnecessary commands. Just as the brain needs sleep to re-sort information taken in during the day, we need occasional layoffs from the skills we use the most to reorganize command loops. It gives the brain a chance to reorder its contents and scrap useless commands.

The reminiscence effect applies to movement abilities. You won't come back from a layoff with more power or endurance. But if you've been climbing without a time-off period for a long time, your technique can come back *stronger* than it was when you stopped. By streamlining command loops, a period of time off is sometimes the only way out of a technique plateau.

During a reminiscence period, it's important not to use your climbing engrams. Distance yourself from climbing: no climbing videos, no mental training, no easy bouldering. But stay active. Just as an injury must get some stimulus to recover, research suggests that command loops reorganize best when you use the brain centers involved. The best way to do this without reinforcing climbing command loops is by doing nonclimbing coordination-dependent activities. Engaging in other sports that use strength and balance keeps these centers active.

If you have occasional week-long breaks from climbing, your brain probably has plenty of time to reorganize its loops without a layoff. But if you climb full-time, you shouldn't go more than a year without a layoff period of several weeks or more. What you lose physically is minimal and easily recovered; what you stand to gain technically (not to mention motivationally) is vital to your climbing.

SUMMARY

The physiology of coordination has implications for how best to train technique. Specifically:

- Engrams are best acquired in ideal conditions, then made stress-proof by using them repeatedly in progressively more adverse conditions.

- Scrutinizing technique is most easily done with a partner.
- You can use other sports to benefit your climbing.
- Ongoing technical learning requires time-off periods.

By framing your technique training around these fundamental principles, you provide yourself the best conditions for improvement.

4. TECHNIQUE TRAINING: PRACTICE

Technique training is about learning how the body moves. It aims to provide you with the experience you need to read the rock right and attack moves with the most efficient sequence, body position, and style.

The lack of a developed language in the young sport of climbing restricts the possible depth of written discussion of movement technique. We'll do what we can in the pages that follow by pointing the way to areas worth examining in your climbing. But recognize that there's no substitute for actual climbing. It is only through practice that these ideas will impact how you climb.

Before delving into this chapter, remember that there's no secret technique or style that guarantees success on all routes. The most successful climbers are good at every area of technique. Extra skill in one area will never completely make up for weaknesses in another. You benefit most by developing the techniques you don't have or are worst at.

We'll examine first the specific skill areas at which climbers need practice. The second half of the chapter describes climbing exercises that can help you develop your ability in these areas.

TECHNICAL SKILL AREAS

Just as different parts of your body need strengthening to improve at climbing, so do different areas of technique. And just as

When it comes to style and technique in climbing, the bottom line is, if it works, do it. The final judge of what makes good technique is what gets you up harder routes with less effort. A veteran climber steeped in the dogma of the seventies once claimed, "Climbing is too noble for lunges." Fortunately, high-brow judgments about one technique or another crumble to dust when that technique serves climbers on the hardest on-sights and redpoints.

people have strengths and weaknesses in different parts of their bodies, they also have different natural aptitudes for particular technical areas.

To become aware of the strong and weak areas of your technique, consider the different elements discussed below. We'll begin by looking at hand and footwork and how you use these connections to the rock. Next we'll expand our focus to see how body positioning affects climbing. Finally we'll look at some movement techniques focusing on how hand, foot, and body positioning operate in motion. In each category we'll explore several techniques, consider why they're valuable, and judge which of the exercises to come can be helpful for improving them.

Hand and Footwork

Since your hands and feet maintain your contact with the rock, your skills with them are crucial. Because of the wide variety of surfaces on which people climb, you need to have *diversity* in these skills. The more breadth you have in your ability to use different hand and foot positions, the more likely your success on any route.

Hands and Holds

When gripping holds, the positions of your fingers fall into three categories: closed crimp, open crimp, and extended grip.

In the closed crimp position, the fingers are contracted to their limit across the second joint, while the first joint is typically open to or beyond its limit. The thumb often grabs over the index finger. Force applied to holds concentrates at the tips of the fingers. By requiring the greatest direction change from the tendons crossing the second joint, this position is the most stressful to the ligaments there. It also imposes the most stress on the cartilage and other structures that maintain the first joint's position.

A classic closed crimp.

A closed crimp.

Open crimps.

In an open crimp, the fingers contract across the second joint at a ninety-degree or wider angle. The thumb either dangles or grips crystals or irregularities lying below the finger edge. This position is not as effective at concentrating force at the tips of the fingers, making it less useful on tiny holds. On half-digit or larger holds, however, concentrating force closer to the lip of the hold (shortening the lever length to the second joint) can reduce the force necessary across the second joint. With the angle at the second joint more open, this position is intermediate in its stress on the second joint ligaments and easier on the first joint.

In the extended grip position, the second joint is contracted little if at all. Contraction across the first joint does the grabbing. For the first two joints of the fingers (those most stressed by a closed crimp position), this position is the least injury prone. However, injuries in this position are not uncommon because it's the

position most commonly used in one- or two-finger pockets. Climbers with tightened forearm muscles also risk injury because this position uses the muscle-tendon units at close to their full extension.

Since nonclimbers are normally strongest in tightly crimped positions, they typically begin climbing preferring crimps and avoiding open positions. Climbers solidify such preferences into ruts by climbing most often with their dominant position. Since strength is specific to position, their grip strength improves only in the dominant position, furthering the strength discrepancy between it and their weaker positions. The crimp position stresses the joints more than do open positions, increasing the risk of injury. Although many climbers only feel comfortable crimping, we know top climbers who climb almost exclusively open-handed.

Your comfort with different finger positions will expand or limit your options in climbing as much as your skill with different body positions will. Unfortunately,

Classic extended grip position.

Extended grip on a sloped hold.

No one grip style suits all types of holds. Different features have particular positions that require the least energy to hold. A climber skilled at many positions can share fatigue among them during a climb (see Tactics). And by spreading the stress of climbing across a broad array of positions, hands and forearms can tolerate more climbing with less risk of injury.

The infinite diversity of holds makes hard and fast rules about hand positions inappropriate. Personal characteristics like joint length can make two different climbers prefer different positions on the same hold. The goal to strive for is to be equally comfortable with all positions. Handwork can be improved using almost any of the exercises listed later in this chapter. Just keep in mind the principles of technique training by learning new positions in slower, more controlled types of climbing, then gradually bringing these new positions into the faster, more stress-proofing types of exercises.

Footwork

Climbers have traditionally lumped almost everything relating to the use of the lower

Edging a small hold.

until you feel comfortable with the different positions, it's difficult to compare them objectively; as a result, many climbers develop skill at only one grip style.

body under the term "footwork." Good footwork involves using your lower body to take on the most efficient amount of the effort necessary to get up a climb. It allows us to conserve our limited upper body strength by transferring work from our weaker upper body to the bigger muscle groups down below. Many of these muscles routinely support our weight for extended periods when we walk or stand. Getting the most out of the lower body in climbing requires a more refined use than most of us are used to.

The challenge of footwork stems from the fact that our feet are estranged from our awareness by shoes, habit, and distance. Learning how to place one's hands on holds requires fewer lessons, because we're used to paying close attention to sensations in our hands, and we feel directly how different grips work. Wearing shoes for most of our lives has reduced our sensitivity to our feet, and the old clunky climbing boots did little to change that.

Learning good footwork begins by paying close attention to your feet. Listen to the signals they send you, and you'll learn new ways of using them. Since good footwork represents the sum of many smaller skills, improving it requires first identifying which of these you're weak at.

For example, some people have skill with a wide variety of features but lack the ability to regulate the force they exert and hold it within a narrow range. They need to concentrate on developing the control to apply a specific amount of force with their feet and to hold that force steady.

To analyze your footwork, consider the following subskills. You'll spot your deficiencies more readily with these categories as a guide. Having a specific area of footwork to focus on will make improving an easier task.

■ **Feature-specific Ability.** Climbers use a full spectrum of rock features (slopes, edges, pockets, cracks) on a variety of angles. Each involves different combinations of calf, ankle, and toe strength for pushing, pulling, and gripping with the feet, as well as the coordination to control these positions. There are subtleties to using each type of foothold that you can learn only through experience.

■ **Precision.** With precise footwork, you place your feet on the best facet of the hold rather than just trying to stand up on whatever your foot stops on as you slide it onto a feature. And you use the most appropriate portion of your shoe to stand on it.

Foot technique for steep climbing requires skill at turning your foot with exactness so you can pivot on a hold without slipping from it as you turn to face toward the opposite side.

■ **Force Control.** Force control refers to the ability to apply an appropriate and consistent degree of force to a hold in a specific direction. On a difficult route, for example, you may need at least twenty pounds of pressure from a particular foothold to make a move, but the hold may accommodate only twenty-five pounds of force before your rubber gives way. Successfully using this hold requires a steady and controlled use of footwork.

■ **Flagging.** Climbing situations don't always provide good footholds for both feet. Even if they do, it's often more efficient to use one foothold while making a hand move and simply stabilize with the other foot.

Flagging involves using one foot for torsional stability by propping it against the wall. It requires no footholds since it uses force directed toward the wall to stabilize the body. This counteracts the tendency to pivot when one's center of gravity lies to one side of the imaginary line that connects the hand locking off and the weight-bearing foot. Flagging often involves crossing the unweighted foot behind or in front of the weighted leg to counter "barn-dooring."

Nearly all the exercises discussed later in this chapter can benefit these subskills of footwork if you make them a priority in your climbing. Again, seeking out the widest variety of rock features, climbing styles, and conditions will do the most for your foot technique.

Footwork is an inseparable part of the broader technique you use in climbing. If you don't know how to position your upper body most effectively for a particular style of climbing, you won't know what to look for with your feet. What may seem like poor footwork may simply be an overall lack of ability at a particular style of climbing. Let's turn our focus to the rest of the body.

Body Positioning

What is the effect of body position on the moves we make in climbing? With any set of holds, there may be several physical orientations by which you can accomplish the moves. But all orientations don't require the same effort. Some positions make use of bigger muscles, better leverage in our limbs, and better angles of pull on the holds. These positions have mechanical advantages over others. Since the effects of less efficient choices are cumulative during a pitch, the most successful climber makes the best choices among possible moves.

Mechanical Advantage

If we look closely, we see that body position affects mechanical advantage in two ways. First, the body's position relative to a hold affects the *direction of force* you can apply to it, and hence how effectively you can grip it. It's hard to pull down, for example, on a side-pull that's directly over your head. But it could be a useful hold if the body were positioned to the side of it. Even subtle alterations in the body's position affect how functional a given hold is.

Second, the body's position determines *biomechanical advantage*. Position your fingers as if you were crimping a hold. With the other hand, pull on them to test their strength. Then do the same test with your wrist bent in toward your forearm. Your

Max flagging to the inside.

fingers are much weaker in the latter position. This shows how body position affects our strength. Although no one climbs with bent wrists, many use body positions that sacrifice biomechanical advantage.

Biomechanical advantage and direction of force interplay on all types of terrain. However, you can't always maximize both at once. On up-to-vertical rock, optimizing direction of force on the handholds usually takes precedence, because usability of tiny handholds is often the limiting factor on such routes. On steep rock, where upper-body strength is more important, biomechanical advantage frequently dictates body position.

Techniques that yield optimal body position on one type of climbing can hinder you on another. On true slabs, for example, leaning in sabotages the use of footholds. Consider a slab that's thirty degrees off vertical. When the body stands upright away from the rock, the direction of force on footholds will point toward the rock at nearly thirty degrees. With this angle of force on the rock, even minor flaws in its surface make usable footholds. Leaning inward reduces this angle and changes the direction of force, making footholds more tenuous.

On near-vertical rock, however, leaning out from the wall typically compromises the direction of force on handholds. It increases the outward component of pull on handholds, making them feel less positive. To succeed at this type of climbing, the climber weighs what positions allow the best use of the holds and considers the angles of pull their particular orientations suggest. The most effective positions typically reduce outward pull on the hands and improve direction of force on handholds by keeping the body close to the rock. If you're flexible, turning out your legs allows you to do this while still using footholds on both sides of you. Climbing "tall" works better for less flexible climbers—keeping the knees straightened out below or to the side instead of between the climber and the rock. Maintaining a frontal upper body orientation also keeps the trunk's mass closer to the wall.

This frontal approach that is so effective on vertical climbing doesn't work on overhanging walls. Steep climbing differs because your body falls outward from the wall. With gravity pulling you *away* from the surface you climb (rather than downward parallel to it), it's not enough for your points of contact with the rock to support you vertically and let your body be close to the rock. To climb, your hands and feet must hold you in toward the wall.

On near-vertical rock, turnout keeps the body close to the wall, minimizing outward pull on handholds.

Combatting the outward pull not present on less steep rock changes your arms' orientations of pull relative to your body, requiring more upper arm, shoulder, back, and core strength. As a result, finding the positions of maximum biomechanical advantage is critical, and the climber must constantly consider what body position will allow him to use holds with the least strength. This necessitates positions and techniques inappropriate to lower-angle climbing.

Body Tension

Optimizing direction of force on steep rock requires body tension, the tautness running through the body linking one point of contact with the rock to another. If you think of holding two side-pulls facing away from each other, you can imagine the tension running through the body between your two hands. Effective use of each side-pull depends on the tension that results from holding the other.

Body tension refers to this transfer of power through the torso where force derived from one hold enhances the use of another. On overhanging rock, for example, tension created by pulling the lower body toward the rock with your feet improves the usability of handholds. By changing the direction of pull, the handholds feel more positive because your body weight is no longer hanging straight down from them. Just as rigidity keeps a bridge straight between points of contact with the ground, body tension maintained by your core muscles keeps your body from sagging, holding your central body mass toward the overhanging wall, suspended between points of contact.

Many climbers maintain tension only between their arms. They don't realize that tension can also run through their core, connecting feet to hands. Even when a climber places his feet well on all the holds, if he uses only a pushing force directed from his feet toward his body, the directions of force he can apply to handholds are limited to gravity's whim.

Body tension requires using the lower body similarly to the way we use our arms and hands, and it demands strong core muscles to transfer forces between the lower and upper body. Think of your feet as tools for positioning your core in three-dimensional space to optimize your orientation for the moves you must make.

Twist-locks

Twist-locks involve turning the upper body to face the hold being locked off. If you're locking your left arm to reach with your right, you would face your torso to the left, turning your chest toward the left arm.

Max losing body tension.

Your feet are tools that position your core in space to give you the best orientation possible.

Twist-locks provide reach and strength advantages. Steep climbing lock-off strength varies dramatically with body position. The body is strongest at lock-offs when the torso turns toward the hold being locked. Twisting your lock-offs also adds signifi-cantly to your reach by positioning the shoulder of your reaching arm closer to its destination.

Many climbers remain facing the wall they're climbing regardless of which arm they're locking off. Pullup training rein-

A good twist-lock. Twisting lengthens reach and requires less strength. Note how using the left foot's outside edge allows the whole body to roll to the side.

Trying the same move without a twist. All the reach power must come from the upper arm and shoulder.

forces this bad habit. Unfortunately, such frontal lock-offs are usually a mistake on anything past vertical.

Outside Edging

Now let's consider what to do with the feet during twist-locks. Next time you climb a ladder, lean it against a wall and climb its underside. Notice which hand and foot move together. Most people weight diagonally opposed limbs together. Nordic skiers call this "diagonal stride," and it's the normal mode of walking. An example of diagonal stride on rock is when the left hand and right foot support the body while the right hand reaches and the left foot either dangles or flags for stability.

Because vertical climbing doesn't involve outward pull on the body, diagonal strides are often no more stable than parallel strides, in which both limbs on one side of the body support body weight. On steeper climbing, however, gravity's pull away from the wall makes it easy for the body to pivot outward like a misaligned barn door. In these situations, diagonal strides have a big advantage.

Using diagonals on steep walls feels balanced because tension between diagonal points of contact passes through one's center of gravity. As a result, diagonal strides are more stable and resist barn-door pivoting. By contrast, the imaginary line of force connecting two parallel points of contact on a wall (right hand to right foot, for instance) passes outside one's body, and the center of gravity will always try to pivot to a position below this line. Therefore, when you can choose between diagonal and parallel contacts with the rock, diagonals will best maintain stable body tension on overhanging climbing.

To combine this with the twisting of the upper body required for twist-locks, you use the outside edge of the diagonal foot. For example, to twist into a left arm lock-off, standing on the outside edge of the right foot orients the body to the left and minimizes barn-dooring. This confers a biomechanical and reach advantage over a frontal orientation. The other foot might be inside edging on a hold, flagging for stability, or just dangling.

The key to outside edging is knowing when to use which foot. You outside edge with the foot diagonally opposed to the hand that's locking off. Let your handholds and hand sequences dictate what your feet do. And don't feel you must always use the biggest or best holds. The *location* of each

foot placement and the body position it allows are usually more important than its size.

As you reach alternately with both hands, you may end up facing to one side and then the other as you ascend. As a result, a climber ascending overhanging rock looks distinctly different from one frontally ascending a near-vertical wall.

In addition to optimizing twist-locks, outside edging offers its own biomechanical advantages. When two edges face each other on a wall, dropping one knee to outside edge one of the holds enables you to "chimney" between them. With a dropped knee, you can apply strong opposition force between footholds too close to stem with open knees. This can lock your lower body close to the wall while you make an arm move. Again, your hands typically prescribe which way

A good twist-lock.

Performing the same move with a frontal orientation is much harder.

Twisting the lock keeps the body closer to the wall.

With parallel points of contact (right hand and foot), the left foot must flag to counteract the body's tendency to pivot out and around to the right.

you face (and thus which knee you drop) on such a move.

For the many people who normally climb frontally, learning to use the outside edge and twist-lock techniques can dramatically improve climbing technique on steep rock.

Exercises that emphasize slow, controlled kinesthetic awareness are best for learning about effective body positioning. Static and slow-motion climbing, blind climbing, and animal imitations can all be helpful in this regard. (These exercises are described in detail later in this chapter.)

Movement Techniques

The following techniques are not separate from those already discussed, but they emphasize a different aspect of movement: *efficiency.* How can we use the techniques already discussed most effectively?

Dynamic Moves

A dynamic move exploits momentum to reach the next hold. Typically, a thrusting motion in the body initiates momentum, which then propels the body toward its target. The body is in motion as the reach is made.

Dynamic movements eliminate the need to hold a difficult position statically. As a result, they save you energy. By using momentum, they also allow you to reach for holds that are beyond your static range of reach.

We'll have more to say about dynamic technique throughout this chapter.

The Deadpoint

A deadpoint is a precision type of dynamic move first refined to an art by Wolfgang

A twist-lock on steep rock. The dangling foot's weight helps roll the body into the twist.

A more stable twist-lock uses diagonal points of contact (left hand and right foot), with the left foot flagging for balance.

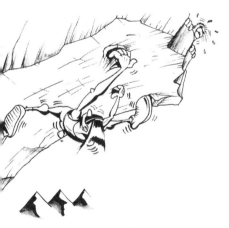

Dropping one knee allows you to twist a lock-off even when stemming between opposed footholds.

Twisting in an undercling move.

Güllich. Like other dynamic movements, deadpoints use momentum to get the body to the next hold. But a deadpoint controls the momentum so that it dies out at just the perfect moment for grabbing the next hold. The name refers to the brief point at the top of an arc of motion where momentum has died out and the body is temporarily motionless before starting its downward fall.

This instant is a moment of opportunity for a climber. During its brief interval, you can latch holds with a minimum amount of energy, since your body is momentarily motionless. Deadpointing thus allows you to catch holds that lie beyond your static reach but that are too small to lunge for.

This technique requires launching a precise movement so that the deadpoint in the arc occurs at the desired position in space relative to the next hold. To do this you have to develop controlled momentum in your body and learn how to use it.

On steep routes where climbers must reach from small holds to small holds, deadpointing is often a must. Even on easier ground, deadpointing moves instead of climbing them statically can help you conserve the extra energy static lock-offs would demand.

See the one-arm traverse exercise later in the chapter for more on dynamic and deadpoint technique. When trying difficult dynos or deadpoints, taking weight off can be helpful, and exaggerating the techniques on easy ground will help to develop the motor engrams for more dynamic movement.

Pacing

"When on-sight climbing, which is more efficient: taking the time to figure out the best possible sequence, or trying the first one that comes to mind, hoping to get out of a difficult section more quickly?" "Should I take advantage of a rest that gives me only slight recovery?" Such questions have to do with one's pacing on a route.

Though many people consider pacing an appropriate concern in sports where time is a consideration, few apply it to climbing. Don't make this mistake. Different routes can impose widely varying time pressures based on the nature of the climbing and on other characteristics of the route. As a result, distinct paces suit different types of climbing. And our changing levels of endurance and strength also dictate particular pacing strategies (see Tactics for more on this).

Inappropriate pacing can be disastrous. At the 1991 World Cup in Nürnberg, for example, the women's semifinal was steeply overhanging for all but the final fifteen feet (which were vertical). On a route like this, with few intermediate holds to consider, the faster you get through the moves, the more energy and power you save for the rest of the route. It's no surprise that the relative standings of the women we analyzed on this route correspond almost exactly to how much time they took climbing through it.

Order of Performance	Time Taken from the Beginning to the Lip
Isabelle Patissier	1:15 minutes
Robyn Erbesfield	1:18 minutes
Susi Good	1:17 minutes
Lynn Hill	1:46 minutes
Bobbi Bensman	3:29 minutes

By contrast, climbing too quickly limits you on routes that don't drain power and endurance as fast. Since there's little to lose by taking extra moments to figure out the best possible sequence, taking your time is a plus on such routes. At the predominantly vertical 1989 Snowbird International Competition, winner Didier Raboutou climbed slowest of all the competitors, topping out more than thirty minutes after leaving the ground.

The key to effective pacing lies in being versatile and understanding what's appropriate in different situations. The best way to learn about pacing is by experimenting on different types of climbs. Trying paces that are both faster and slower than those you normally use helps you discover your optimal pace.

EXERCISES

Nothing could be more obvious: to improve your technique, you've got to work on your technique. Yet amazingly few climbers really understand the implications of this simple fact.

"Can't I just practice technique when I'm doing routes at the crag?" Bruno asks. Of course he can try, but unless he's prepared for a gradual learning process, his rate of progress might disappoint him. There are good reasons why several years of his normal approach haven't yet given Bruno good technique.

Climbing at the crag, Bruno's mind is filled with a myriad of concerns: "Will I make it to the top? Is the protection okay? Are they watching me? Am I looking good? Did Fred flash this route?" There are just too many competing interests for him to focus on the subtleties of movement. The last thought he would entertain as he gasps his way past a crux is, "Gee, I wonder what creative techniques might have worked better on that last move."

As we discussed in the last chapter, stress reverts us back to our most ingrained movement patterns. To work with new patterns, we must reduce some of the normal challenges in order to clear space for learning technique.

Learning occurs best when you remove distracting and nagging demands on your awareness so you can focus on feeling the movement and dynamics of your body. The

Climbing Walls

Versatility and economy make climbing walls with modular holds ideal for technical exercises. You can build them almost anywhere, even on a shoestring budget. We know one climber who put one on the underside of his kitchen table!

The lack of intermediate features often requires sequences using specific techniques. By rotating, moving, or changing holds you can fine-tune a problem to your needs. But you don't *have* to change anything that's there. Just look for a set of holds defining the kind of moves you want to work on.

Through trial and error, you'll isolate exact hold layouts that call for particular techniques. In the process you'll get practice experimenting with sequences and visualizing body positions on climbing walls. You'll also be doing climbing-specific strength training.

Make up whatever arbitrary rules are necessary to make a good sequence. On rising boulder problems, for example, "tracking" requires that only holds formerly used by the hands are permitted as footholds.

Try making problems that exploit your partner's weaknesses, and encourage him or her to do the same for you. Then you'll both have boulder problems personally tailored to your biggest needs.

Jibé Tribout warming up on his backyard climbing wall.

technique exercises in this chapter will help you do this.

A technique exercise consists of nothing more than climbing with one or two technical issues as your focus. You can do this with any aspect of technique. The exercises are games or made-up challenges, often unrealistic compared with the normal act of climbing, that highlight particular techniques. Success, failure, and falling are all irrelevant in these exercises. You strive only to learn technique. Remember that you'll have to step back a notch from the grades you normally find challenging to focus on new technique issues.

The following are some technique exercises we know of. Some may seem silly or nonserious, but don't underestimate them. These exercises are more than just entertainment—they're refined approaches that can revolutionize your climbing.

Style Exercises

There are many different styles of climbing movement. Some climbers are aggressive on rock, others are timid. Some climb frontally, others twist from side to side as they reach. Some climb flexibly, usually with both feet on the rock, others are danglers who rarely have more than one foot on a hold at a time. Some climb statically, others dyno even the easiest moves. Where some climb tall, others bunch themselves up.

There are successful climbers who embody each of these styles. But those who are good at the widest variety of terrain adapt their climbing style to the needs of the route they're on.

In general, our style results from our personal profile of strengths and weaknesses. Strong climbers, for example, sometimes use less care with their footwork; endurance climbers move more slowly, taking time to find the least power-demanding sequence. Our style results from our skills—but it also contributes to the development of our skills and deficits. Strength climbers avoid technical routes, and technique climbers shy away from strength-dependent routes. Even on the same route,

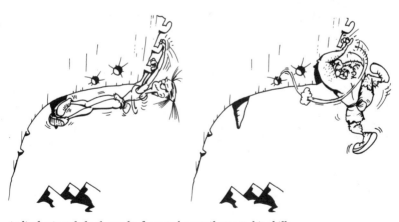

A climber's style both results from and contributes to his skills.

the strength climber will find a muscle sequence; the technical climber, a tricky way through. Our personal style thus confines the development of our abilities to particular directions. By sticking to a personal style, climbers can dig themselves into a rut.

It's helpful, therefore, to make deliberate efforts to climb in styles contrary to those you normally use. The following are some useful exercises to try.

Speed

Speed climbing helps you stress-proof the techniques you have and learn to make quick selections between them. It also helps you learn about pacing. Climbers often find that speed climbing a route that's normally strenuous for them is *less* pumping than climbing it at their normal pace. Getting comfortable at speed climbing broadens the arsenal of paces you bring to the crags, granting you more versatility on different rock types. After getting used to the rapid rate of decision making and muscle firing that speed climbing requires, your normal pace will feel snail-like by comparison.

Start on an easy route with obvious holds and sequences. Once you've done it a couple times, try speed climbing on styles of routes that you're normally more hesitant on. Timing your ascents and comparing with your friends helps you isolate the specific factors involved in speed.

Slow Motion

Slow-motion climbing highlights the subtle aspects of movement and the transitions of forces and weight between moves. When climbing in slow motion you have the time to be aware of every part of your movement. You can sense the weight shifts, coordination of body parts, and sequences of muscle involvement that happen too quickly to follow at a normal climbing pace. Mistakes usually hidden by their brevity become obvious.

One Foot On

Many climbers with excessively static technique insist on having both feet on the rock before moving a hand to the next hold. If you're one of these climbers, you'd benefit from breaking this pattern by doing technique exercises where you climb with just one foot on the wall at a time. It's okay to have both feet on while walking your feet

Hans Florine winning the 1991 World Speed-climbing Championships.

up to holds, but dangle or flag one of them when you make your hand moves.

Again, choose routes or boulders that are easy for you, and make this your focus. You'll learn a lot about how foot positioning affects balance.

Animal Imitations

Different types of routes suit very different styles of climbing. Steep bucket climbing, for example, benefits from feeling at ease when your body swings and using this to your advantage. Barn-door laybacking and technical slab climbing, on the other hand, suffer from the same approach. These differences in approach are more than can be described by a few simple body rules like "be dynamic" or "don't swing." They involve a wide array of complex movement patterns. As a result, many people find they can more easily switch from one pattern to another by imitating animals that move in characteristic ways.

Imagine how a monkey swings from branch to branch. No single move is kinesthetically independent of the move that precedes or follows it. The last move's momentum carries into the next. Even if he pauses before a move, he doesn't start it randomly. He waits until the point of the swing at which momentum will help him. Picturing and feeling this before starting up an overhanging bucket climb where momentum is important can help more than a dozen reminders to yourself about how to use your body.

Or picture a lizard climbing a near-vertical wall. Arms and legs to the side, his center of gravity stays close to the wall. His head goes from side to side with each move to keep his weight positioned over

his feet. Each move is quick, deliberate, and cringe-free.

Envision a cat's stealthy approach to its prey followed by a burst of speed to down it. This attitude can help you sneak up on a crux before fatigue finds you, saving your power and aggression for the moves that require it.

A snake slithers around, under, and between obstacles. We know a top climber who pictures himself doing the same through hard sections of an on-sight. Climbing is a game for the devious: he who can slink his way through, around, or out of cruxes wins.

Static Cling

Static climbing simply means climbing without using momentum to reach holds or position your body. When climbing statically, your body should not swing or move when you lift a hand or foot off one hold to reach the next. You position your body *first* so that in making the move, only your hand travels. Static climbing ends up being a series of static positions that, though not the most efficient way to climb, can teach you valuable lessons about climbing movement.

Climbing statically reveals how subtle shifts in weight or force affect the body's mechanical advantage; this helps teach the optimal body positions from which to reach for holds. The body positioning you learn about applies to more than just static climbing. In a well-done dyno, your body passes *through* the positions of maximum mechanical advantage you find yourself assuming to make an efficient static move.

Lock-off climbing is a variation on static climbing. Before gripping each subsequent hold, you float your hand over it without weighting it for two to five seconds. This

Rest positions.

accentuates the role of strength in static climbing.

Another variation on static climbing develops your skill at finding rest positions amidst hard moves. On each hold you grab, find a rest position in which you can chalk and shake the other hand. Although this isn't a style of climbing to strive for, the exercise can teach you a lot about resting and recovering on difficult terrain.

Dynamic Motion

Beginners and veterans alike often cringe when their body moves while reaching for a handhold. Old maxims like "maintain three points of contact with the rock" and "never fall" contributed to the notion that good technique consists of static, hesitant climbing.

Nothing could be farther from the truth. Bringing more movement into our climbing makes hard moves quicker and easier. Dynamic exercise help you escape from the limitations of excessively static technique.

Dynamic climbing involves body momentum in movements. To practice it, get on a route that's easy for you, and make as many

To develop momentum you must first draw back away from your target.

of the hand moves as possible with a dynamic style. Even if you could easily make a move statically, initiate momentum in your body so that you're moving as your hand reaches for the next hold. Once you're used to this, feel for the deadpoint in your movement, and practice catching holds during its golden instant.

Start on routes with large and easy-to-grab holds. By getting used to moving dynamically on easy ground, you familiarize yourself with the use of momentum. Then gradually transfer what you learn to more

and more tenuous situations. Eventually you can climb dynamically on routes where smaller holds require precision. Note, however, that crack climbs and routes where you have to fiddle to take a hold don't suit this type of exercise.

Read the following section for a more detailed look at dynamic technique.

One-arm Traverses

One-arm traversing isolates many of the principles of dynamic movement into a simple exercise helpful to climbers uncomfortable with it. Once proficient at this technique, climbers also can use one-arm traversing to train power-endurance. Try it first on easy vertical traverses with big handholds.

Momentum is the currency of dynos. Although you don't always want a lot of it, skill at dynos requires learning how to recruit momentum and how to make use of it once you've got it.

Newcomers to one-arm traversing tend to dyno only with their arms. They position their body close to the wall, then try to shoot their arm to the next hold before their body has time to fall too far backward. Better technique comes when the motion involves the *body's* momentum. Because it has high mass, your abdominal area is a good place to initiate momentum. As with a bow and arrow, developing momentum requires first drawing back away from your target. Next you thrust your abdomen toward the wall, transferring its momentum up your body in a wavelike motion toward your target hold.

For practice, try maximizing your hand's "hang time" between holds. Strive to look like you're doing each dyno in slow motion.

One-arm traverses can be stressful to the shoulders and elbows. Keep some bend in your arm when you catch holds so the pull on your arm is supported by muscle tension, not joints. And remember to traverse both directions with each arm.

Exaggeration

Often mistakes occur because you aren't aware of what's going on kinesthetically. When other methods fail, exaggeration can make your errors conscious and obvious and therefore easier to correct. Either exaggerating it yourself or getting someone else to exaggerate your error can help you see what you're doing wrong.

Contrast your exaggerated mistake with an exaggerated version of the way you want to do the move. If you must fall off to effectively exaggerate, do so.

Faking It

Bruno stands on a small edge and a smear, sloping holds in each hand. He winces at having nothing positive to muscle up on, realizing several more nonpositive moves await. One look at him and you know he's in trouble: his feet tremble slightly, and his whole body is tightly gripped by a physical and mental cringe. He makes another

Momentum flows up your body in a wavelike motion.

move, but in his high-tension slow motion, a foot pops off and he's airborne.

This cowering reaction to thin moves is the first reaction of most beginners, but it carries the seeds of its own downfall. When you cower you move slowly and rigidly, and you typically tremble. Trembling legs maximize foot creep off bad holds. Procrastinated movements increase fatigue. In an unrelaxed body, one foot popping off a hold typically brings down the house, since a tightened body cannot adjust quickly to a new system of pressure and tension.

This body language represents the expectation and anxiety of falling that such insecure climbing prompts. Sometimes the anticipation of a foot or hand popping off a hold half-paralyzes us long before it ever happens. Yet the expectation of doom shows in every gesture. Bruno presses upward bit by bit on wobbly feet, never using his full extension. This inappropriate body language is the most common cause of failure on such routes.

Insecure climbing requires a relaxed and deliberate confidence. Since insecure climbing demands something opposite to what you feel when you're doing it, trick yourself into climbing it well by faking it. *Act* as if the holds feel big; climb as you would if they were. Move like you expect success, even if you don't believe it. It helps you relax unnecessarily contracted muscles that stiffen climbers in such situations. This helps you move more fluidly and reduces the tendency to tremble. Faking it also minimizes your hesitation between moves, reducing your time in the insecure sections. On thin climbing, you won't be thrusting up on holds. But stand up on them deliberately and you'll make the best of your chances.

Weight Off

It gets frustrating. You're up against a bouldering move you just can't do, yet you don't know how to get better at it.

One way to work on such a move is to have a partner support part of your weight while you do the move. Have him or her take off as much weight as necessary for you to do it well. Then, as you gather experience on the move through this approach, gradually reduce the amount of aid. On moves that would otherwise be too hard for you, it gives you very specific training that allows you to practice succeeding on the move rather than failing repeatedly.

To take weight off someone else, keep these pointers in mind. Support the climber near his center of gravity, pushing upward on his lower back area with your hand. Keep the amount of force constant throughout the movement—don't press harder at the difficult part of the move. Maintain a consistent orientation to the force you provide.

Uninterrupted Climbing

Many climbers who are inhibited on rock gain from uninterrupted thirty-minute climbing sessions, which we'll discuss in the endurance training chapter. After doing several thirty-minute sessions, these climbers experience a springy fluidity in their movement on rock. Their movement patterns reflect a relaxed "letting go" that characterizes trust in the instincts held in their engram repertoires. A feeling of fluid lightness results.

A climber's inhibitions are the biggest barrier to this letting go. Thirty-minute sessions break that inhibition by desensitizing him to the basic act of climbing. When you climb continuously beyond a certain time threshold, your body starts dropping its apprehensions and learning to move efficiently. Climbers develop a certain comfort from having logged extended time on rock and feel they're back on familiar terrain when they climb.

Blindfolded Climbing and Proprioceptive Training

Climbing blindfolded or with closed eyes is another valuable exercise to try on easy and safe ground. Shutting off a channel of information you rely heavily on increases your concentration on forms of information often ignored while climbing.

You'll notice subtle responses in your body that normally hide behind the rush of input from the senses. For example, when many climbers pull hard or cling tightly to a hold, they contract unnecessary muscles in their neck and shoulders or hold their breath. Such reactions that may have gone unnoticed through years of normal climbing stand out behind the darkness of a blindfold.

More important, however, blindfolded climbing helps improve kinesthetic and spatial awareness. For experienced climbers, vision acts as a verifier or calibrator of the body's proprioceptive or "position" sense. But the eyes can only watch one or two holds at a time. An awareness beyond

vision maintains control over the rest of the body. With input from the senses, your mind creates a three-dimensional image of your immediate environment and constructs a mental hologram within which you move. Climbing without sight develops and sharpens this position sense.

Without sight, your kinesthetic awareness has less to compete with for your attention. The quality of movement throughout your body becomes obvious. Are your motions fluid, or does part of your body want to remain rigid while the rest moves? Look for these sticking points in your body that resist complete or fluid motion.

Your spatial awareness also comes to the forefront. At first you may struggle to find and trust footholds. Without the visual crutch, however, you learn to feel their size and angle through your shoes. You take note of the shapes and positions of your handholds, with future use by your feet in mind. Eventually, you can place your feet on holds accurately from your spatial memory of their positions as ex-handholds. To see how training emphasizing proprioception can improve technique, consider the following example.

Four hundred feet above the Crooked River, Max battles gravity on the 73rd move of *Lust Blew It*. With a low two-finger pocket for his right hand and a marginal thumbs-down side-pull overhead for his left. Max's right hand must reach for another two-finger pocket above. Since the side-pull is too poor to allow a static reach for the pocket, the move requires a precise deadpoint with the right hand. To make matters worse, the direction of force the side-pull allows doesn't help the climber pull directly toward the pocket. Mustering effective momentum for the move requires coordinating forces from all four points of contact.

After a couple of tries Max can successfully make the move but his hesitation before deadpointing worries him. He adjusts his body up and down, back and forth, feeling for the position that best coordinates the force vectors acting on him. Finding the optimal orientation and executing this deadpoint takes Max a painfully long time. From his redpoint experience, Max knows that such delays spell failure on strenuous routes.

To eliminate this hesitation and learn to make technically difficult moves with greater fluidity and confidence, Max needs to focus on the crucial line of input to his kinesthetic centers: his proprioceptive awareness. With proprioceptive training, Max would more instinctively find the optimal response to a particular arrangement of holds.

To use proprioceptive training, look for ways to reduce or eliminate the role of sight on practice moves. On a vertical bouldering wall, for example, try spotting the next hold in a sequence, then reaching for it with closed eyes. As you get more comfortable with it, begin doing dynamic moves, where timing must be accurate when grabbing holds. Next, practice double dynamic moves, where both hands reach to a hold at once. After doing the move with sight to calibrate your position sense, close your eyes to make the move on proprioceptive awareness alone. As your proprioceptive senses sharpen you'll find that you can dyno from two separate holds to two different holds without sight. Repeatedly dynoing up and down between two holds or sets of holds

ingrains the proprioceptive awareness of a particular movement.

Be creative! Develop your proprioceptive awareness on different angles, varied holds, and diverse moves. The value of efficient and fluid movement that sharpened proprioceptive sensitivity builds can hardly be overstated. As an advanced technique exercise, proprioceptive training can do for your technique training today what the advent of reactive training ten years ago did for power training.

The Stick Game

Many climbers find it boring to train endurance or power-endurance by bouldering continuously on hold-studded climbing walls. It's easy to get bored continually making up your own moves, and you tend to unconsciously favor types of moves you are already skilled at. Stick training with a partner resolves these problems.

With a pointer, the partner points to holds ahead of the climber to show the sequence of holds he must use. The climber must work out his partner's challenges by continuously solving his sequences. It's valuable because the partner can lead the climber into sequences he would not normally use or emphasize moves representing the climber's weaknesses. And it more closely simulates on-sight climbing, since every move is externally dictated.

The two best ways of stick training are hand sequence and foot sequence. In the first, the partner points to successive handholds, staying one or two moves ahead of the climber. Generally, he indicates which hand the climber must use on each hold, though he also can let some holds be

Stick training.

"matching" holds. He also may restrict the climber to a certain part of a hold ("only the side"). The climber can use any footholds he chooses to accomplish the prescribed hand sequence. In the foot-sequence variant, the partner indicates successive footholds and the climber uses any hand sequence he wants to.

Skilled guiding makes or breaks stick training, since the partner controls the climber's workout. The skilled partner chooses sequences that explore the climber's weaknesses. For power-endurance training, the partner keeps the climber on the verge of failure for extended periods by giving him big holds every time he is getting desperate and leading him back to smaller holds when he's less pumped. The partner can easily "finish him off" after a chosen length of time by not letting him onto rest holds. Or the partner can emphasize local endurance by keeping the climber farther from the point of failure and letting him climb longer.

Mental Training

Mental training seeks to ingrain movement patterns through visualization. It extends your ability to improve by allowing you to practice climbing with neither fatigue nor

Mental training.

risk. Any of the drills mentioned above can be used in mental training provided you have experience with them in reality.

Mental training capitalizes on a mind-body response called the Carpenter Effect. When you vividly imagine a movement or identify closely with a climber you watch, corresponding electrical impulses travel the muscles you would actually use to make the movement. This shows that visualization activates the motor engrams that control movement. Since use solidifies engrams, mental training can improve your technique.

The more vivid your visualization—the more closely your mental training corresponds with reality—the greater transfer you'll have from mind to matter. It helps to get comfortable and to relax before beginning mental training.

Find a comfortable chair and try the following exercise. Think of a boulder problem or short route whose moves you know well. Close your eyes and take some deep breaths while making real the setting of your visualization. Recreate the sounds, smells, and sights that accompany the moves you'll be practicing. Go through any warm-up activities you normally do before climbing. When ready, begin your climb. Pay particular attention to the sensations of your body. Feel your muscles pulling and your weight pressing down on your footholds. Feel how your body plays against gravity to make its moves. Feel individual crystals of rock under your fingers as you take hand-holds; feel the air and your clothes against your skin. Make each move with the ease or awkwardness it normally entails. When you finish, descend by your normal means, take another deep breath, and open your eyes.

To test for the realism of your mental training, compare the time a route takes you mentally with the time required in reality. The better you are in visualizing, the closer you'll come to your actual climbing time.

Mental training also underscores the value of watching good climbers and seeing good technique in action. It explains why there's no faster way to learn than by example. When you see a climber whose technique you'd like to emulate, put yourself in her place as she climbs. *Feel* what her moves must feel like as you watch, and repeat them to yourself after she finishes.

These exercises have proven useful for working on technique. With an experimental

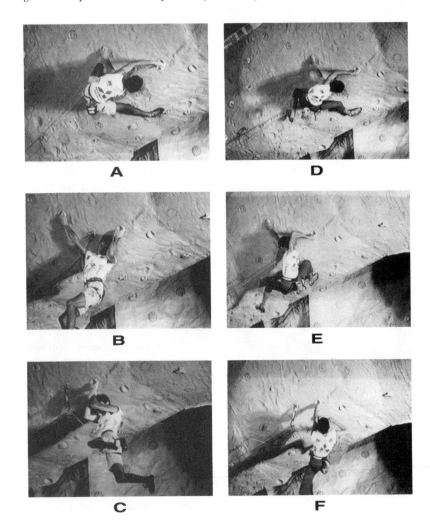

A

D

B

E

C

F

approach to climbing, you'll think of others, and your climbing results will quickly prove them valuable or not. Give them a chance and technique exercises will change the way you climb.

HOW TO BECOME WORLD CHAMPION

Video stills (which are somewhat fuzzy but illustrate our point nicely) from the 1991 World Championships confirm an important lesson. Climbing is a movement-dependent sport.

Over and over the lesson is clear. The cumulative effects of tiny mistakes and inefficiencies have big consequences. The best climber is not necessarily stronger than the rest. He's the one who makes the fewest movement errors. The choices of moves and positions and the speed with which they're made separates climbers.

To see how this occurred at the 1991 World Championships, let's compare the top four finalists to the winner, François Legrand.

Compare photos A–C with photos D–F. Sixteen-year-old Pavel Samoiline (USSR) is the only competitor besides François to do the efficient crossover sequence in the roof traverse (D). But by trying to stay facing the wall while finishing the cross-through sequence (E), he swings violently in coming out of it. He takes so long preparing for this swing and stabilizing after it that his left arm strength is beyond the point of recovery by the time the move is finished (F). See you next year, Pavel.

François minimizes this problem in two ways. First he turns completely away from

the wall to face the audience (B). This unusual position uncrosses his arms so he doesn't swing like Pavel when he releases his right hand. When he does, he grabs his left wrist with his right hand to stabilize the swing and to minimize left arm fatigue while repositioning his body (C).

Missing the crossover forces the powerful Guido Kostermeyer to do a time-consuming hand switch (G). After the crossover, a shortage of footholds on the overhanging wall makes lower body control very difficult. Guido makes the following dyno (J) using tiny footholds that he can't maintain after reaching the hold (K). This forces him to reestablish his grip from a hanging, crucified position—another energy drain.

François avoids this problem by using a figure-four position (H–I), which holds his lower body in to the wall for control without consuming major core strength reserves (H). This move also helps shift his center of gravity from the left to the right handhold (I).

A move later (L), the tired Guido falls victim to a powerful sidecling lock-off. He loses body tension, his left foot slips, and he falls. The second place competitor, Yuji Hirajama, manages to pull off the move using

G

H

J

I

K

Guido's sequence (O). François, by contrast, uses a dropped knee to take advantage of a marginal stemming opportunity on the wall (M). He not only does with ease the move that shut down Guido and gave Yuji a hard time, he even clips in from this position.

For the next move Yuji must swing around and reset his feet (P), whereas François's solution evolves from his previous move, saving him time (N). The time factor cannot be underestimated. By the time Yuji reaches the stalactite (Q), he's spent 90 seconds more than François on the route's increasingly exhausting moves. A few moves later he falls off, his sweat-drenched body indicating that lactic acid has poisoned his muscles and thus his coordination (see page 18, Coordination and Lactic Acid).

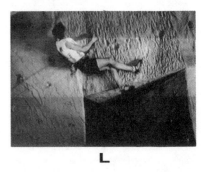

L

François on-sights the 5.13c route and becomes the first official world champion.

Mistakes typically look obvious when you compare them with the optimal move. But recognizing them from an easy chair and avoiding them under the pressure of a climb are two different issues. Only your most prac-

M

O

N

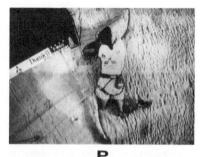

P

ticed movement patterns are available to you in stressful situations.

It almost always feels like you fall off because your fingers open, or you can't hold the hold. But to conclude that you just need more strength misses the essence of climbing. Whether your fingers open or not depends on how you move and how efficiently you've gotten to where you are on a route.

Climbing is a *movement-centered* sport.

Q

5. THE PSYCHOLOGY OF AROUSAL AND PERFORMANCE

"Focus on your goal." "Be confident, relaxed, and smooth." Such self-help platitudes sound great on the surface and often reflect admirable goals. Unfortunately, they offer little in the way of information toward achieving them.

People are so complex that a myriad of factors, some outside the psychological realm, can affect individual psychology. Finding a targeted solution to a psychological issue requires a great deal of knowledge about the person involved; as a result, often only the individual himself or someone who knows him thoroughly possesses the necessary background information.

Although the path out of psychologically rooted sports-performance problems is not a simple one, an understanding of basic psychodynamics can help. We hope to provide a basic understanding of the relationship

between your mind, your body, and your climbing performance. It will then be up to you to incorporate the knowledge only you have about yourself to figure out which of the factors discussed apply most directly to you.

The goal is to become aware of the controllable performance-oriented psychological factors and then, with information from the following chapters, develop techniques for controlling them. Our exploration will center on arousal.

AROUSAL

Consider the relationship between three fundamental processes taking place within us. These three processes form a cooperating inner triad that defines our experience of living. *Psychological processes* relate to your mind and behavior and involve thoughts

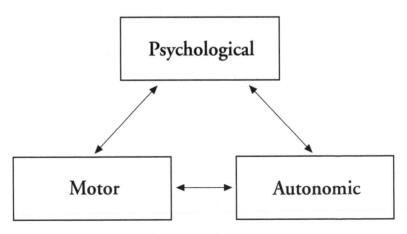

The inner triad processes.

and feelings. *Autonomic processes* automatically control the physiological operating state of the body. They regulate heart rate, breathing, blood vessel size, digestion, and other physiological variables. *Motor processes* include muscle fiber recruitment, coordination, and muscle tone. They affect technique, power, endurance, flexibility, posture, and so on.

Although the ties are not always obvious, each of these processes is inseparably linked to the others. A stimulus or behavior that affects one will have unavoidable effects on the other two. Thus, you can address problems in one process either directly or through the influence of the other two. Because of the intimacy of this *ménage à trois,* psychological and autonomic processes affect the motor processes behind climbing performance.

Performance States

Apart from luck, weather and rock conditions, and other factors outside your control, the processes of the inner triad are the variables that affect your climbing. They constitute all the controllable factors responsible for your ability, and together they define your performance state.

We all know that performance is not constant from moment to moment. You can be climbing at your best one day, then two days later, for no apparent reason, you can feel like you've reverted to a beginners' level. This occurs because the inner triad processes, and hence your performance state, change from moment to moment. Get control of their fluctuations and you'll have control over your climbing performance.

Why does your performance state vary? Because being capable of different operating states makes us more adaptable. Many qualities vital to one task or another are mutually exclusive. For example, states that maximize the power and endurance of your muscles undermine their fine-tuned precision and coordination. Qualities that enhance speed sacrifice accuracy. If you maximize your attention on the immediate present, you can't contemplate strategies for the future.

Because of these trade-offs, there is no single optimum arousal state for all activities. Just as a battleship changes its level of "alert" depending on its situation, so too do the inner triad processes change to create particular performance states.

The body's arousal state is a reflection of the balance of two hormones secreted by the brain's adrenal medulla. These hormones are epinephrine (adrenalin) and norepinephrine. The changing conditions of the inner triad processes reflect the ratio of these two hormones in the body. So although the status of each inner triad process can vary, the three don't change independently of one another. Each process has a characteristic set of responses to different ratios of epinephrine to norepinephrine. A particular status in one process is accompanied by associated tendencies in the others.

When Bruno is psychologically angered by failure, for example, his autonomic and motor systems have particular characteristics. Among other changes, his heart beats faster and his resting muscle tension increases. Since changes in one of the inner triad processes bring about predictable changes in the other two, switching his thoughts to the satisfying aspects of his life will lower Bruno's heart rate and reduce his muscle tone. Alternatively, using techniques to lower his muscle tone or calm his heart will have a pacifying effect on his fiery temper.

Because of these associations, performance states don't vary infinitely but are confined to a narrow range of possibilities based on whether the arousal level is high or low. Let's look at how arousal affects each process.

How Arousal Affects Psychological Processes

Recall your mental state the last time you were in a car accident, a fight, or a dangerous situation against your will. In such situations, perception zooms in on input from the senses. Awareness focuses on the immediate present. Our ability to react quickly and respond instinctively is optimized.

That's certainly helpful in climbing, but there's a trade-off. The immediacy of this awareness quickens our reactions to surprise events at the cost of strategic or planning activity. If you're struggling to cling to the rock because your foot just slipped and you're fifteen feet out from your last protection, you're not planning how best to conserve your energy for the final crux. When all your awareness goes to reacting to the constant stream of input from your senses, there's no consciousness left over for analyzing, predicting, and preparing for anything beyond the moment.

Although climbing can require quick reactions, planning skills are also important. We must anticipate upcoming moves before

launching into them. Preparing your strategy for a pitch as a whole requires even longer-range planning. It is at lower arousal levels that these more intellectual activities are optimized. We consider abstract ideas and contemplate past and future actions best when we're relaxed.

Because of the simultaneous need for both immediate response and longer-term planning, an intermediate level of psychological arousal is best for climbing.

How Arousal Affects Autonomic Processes

As with the psychological effects, the autonomic response to increasing arousal shows a progressive preparation for aggressive physical activity. Low arousal levels reduce blood flow to the muscles. The heart beats calmly. Breathing is slow and shallow. With increasing arousal, these factors speed up. The heart's rate and force of contraction increase, breathing becomes deeper and faster, and blood vessels feeding the muscles open for greater blood flow. Even the blood sugar level rises.

Most of the autonomic responses to arousal favor climbing ability, with one exception. High arousal leads to increased sweating throughout the body, and moistened fingers sacrifice friction against rock.

As a result, climbing benefits from a relatively high but not excessive level of autonomic arousal.

How Arousal Affects Motor Processes

The motor system responds to increasing arousal levels by stoking its fires. Increased arousal raises muscle fiber recruitment and thus increases strength. Fed by the elevated blood supply and blood sugar level discussed above, the muscles are capable of greater endurance. Muscle tone increases.

Although these qualities enhance climbing performance, there's àn important trade-off. With increasing arousal, you lose coordination. So from a motor standpoint, the optimal level of arousal for a particular activity depends on how it blends strength and coordination. For example, although both rely on motor skills, running a race and performing neurosurgery require quite different levels of arousal.

Since climbing is first a technique-dependent sport, excessive arousal cripples climbing performance. Although somewhat different levels of arousal suit different styles of climbs, all require maintaining more co-ordination abilities (and thus lower arousal) than you'd need for a hundred-meter sprint.

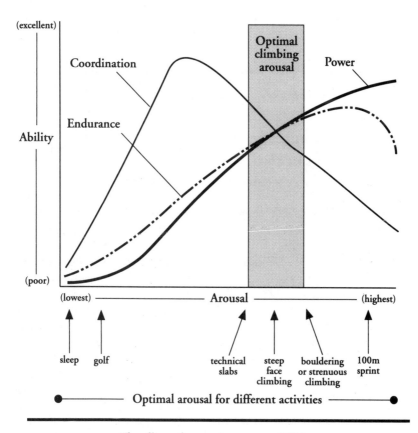

The effects of arousal on motor abilities.

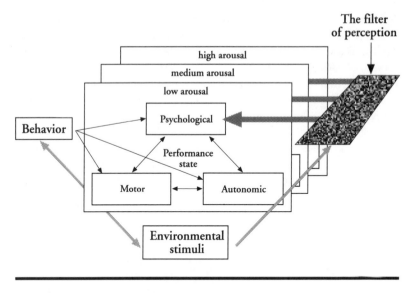

Channels of influence on the performance state.

Factors Influencing the Arousal Level

Each inner triad process is bound to whatever level of arousal you're experiencing. You can't be highly aroused in one process while completely relaxed in another. The optimal arousal level is that which comes closest to meeting your needs in each of the three processes. Looking at all three together, we see that the ideal range of arousal for climbing is intermediate between high and low arousal.

Since we hope to control our state of arousal, we must learn about the avenues by which such control is possible. The actions you do, the thoughts you think, and the countless factors in the environment in which you perform all affect the arousal state of your inner triad. But there are just two channels by which these influences *access* the inner triad: perception and behavior.

Perception

Any stimulus from your environment must pass through the filter of your perceptions to affect your inner processes. Two people may react to a particular stimulus in completely different ways due to differences in how they perceive it. Tell Bruno a route is hard, for example, and he'll become more aroused, because it increases the threat that he might fail. Tell Julia the same and she might become less aroused, thinking the reduced expectations of her friends lowers the pressure on her to succeed. Perceptual differences alter how arousing a given stimulus can be.

The next chapter, Perceptual Approaches to Psychological Control, will look at how perceptual factors affect your arousal and show how attitudes, beliefs, and outlook affect your climbing performance.

Behavior

The actions we perform in response to events around us also affect our arousal. Remember that intentionally altering any of the three inner triad processes affects the hormonal balance underlying arousal, and hence your overall performance state. Top athletes use specific exercises to alter their arousal state by manipulating one or more of the triad process.

Chapter 7, Behavioral Approaches to Psychological Control, will look at these behavioral channels of influence and teach you specific exercises to help you adjust your arousal to the level you desire.

CONCLUSIONS

Climbers have long used anecdotal techniques for psychological support. By repeating certain behaviors on days when they feel "on," they build up associations of success with special phrases, "lucky" pieces of clothing or equipment, and so forth. Although such techniques may help recreate a positive performance state in casual situations, it's dangerous to rely on them for important climbs or competitions.

Fear is a potent arousal raiser and can quickly displace you from a sought-after performance state. Because the above methods don't address arousal, they often fail at the times they're needed most. Most climbers neglect to consider a situation's "threat potential," so they are unprepared for this tendency and become victims of their own emotions.

Since states of arousal impact movement, the fundamental purpose of psychological training is to regulate and control arousal, keeping it at an optimal level. With the information from this chapter in mind, you can monitor whether you're under, over, or appropriately aroused for a given situation.

The only access to our inner world is through two channels: our behaviors and our perceptions. Since we can control our behaviors and influence our perceptions, we can learn to regulate our arousal level and thus attain the performance state we want. By attacking the arousal problem head-on, the techniques discussed in the two following chapters offer more than just a possibility for improved performance. They have proven their effectiveness in a wide array of sports.

6. PERCEPTUAL APPROACHES TO PSYCHOLOGICAL CONTROL

"It's all in your mind." In the case of perception, this saying hits the bull's-eye.

Perceptual effects are more difficult to measure and monitor than the behavioral influences described in the next chapter, and ways of bringing about lasting change in the perceptual arena are less clearly understood. But this doesn't reduce the value to an athlete of pursuing the perceptual approach to psychological control. Experiences we all share and the testimony of innumerable top athletes confirm its worth.

Many of the situations climbers routinely encounter wreak havoc on their performance state. Much of this is due to how these situations are perceived. Through explorations of motivation and expectations, this chapter looks at ways of minimizing these perceptually based problems.

THREAT AND AROUSAL

Wake up with a tiger staring you in the face, and your body must quickly reach an optimal state for sprinting. From thousands of years of evolution, danger has become linked to immediate physical response. As a result, we instinctively react to threats by attaining a state of high arousal. It readies us for bursts of physical exertion.

For a climber, however, all threats don't necessarily involve physical jeopardy. In climbing, for example, threats can involve:

- The environment—an exposed or otherwise intimidating setting.

- The action—a climb that feels tenuous or insecure.
- The self—fear of failure, perceived threats to self-esteem, and so on.

Climbing situations producing these threats don't benefit from the bursts of maximal physical exertion for which high arousal prepares the body. Even in occasions involving true danger, climbing rarely benefits from the heightened arousal to which such conditions lead.

In fact, as we saw in the previous chapter, because high arousal sabotages coordination and reduces other abilities involved in climbing, climbers suffer under its influence. As a result, rarely do climbers need arousal-raising techniques. In the vast majority of situations, climbers need to learn means of reducing their arousal.

Fortunately, the real threat potential of a situation doesn't affect your performance state directly. Arousal hormone balances are based on emotional and conceptual impressions of situations and the things you do in response to them. They are affected no more by external events than by vividly imagined events. If you could enter an extremely threatening situation but experience it emotionally and conceptually as harmless, your arousal level would remain low. Your perceptual "filter" personalizes your reality.

How different situations affect your arousal thus hinges partly on how you view yourself and how you view the world around you. If you're out of control of your mental reactions to events, your inner triad will be a three-ring circus and your arousal level will be hostage to the misperceptions, exaggerations, and overreactions of your mind. On the other hand, if you can exercise control over your perceptions of the external world, you can enter situations that other people would consider intimidating and still maintain your chosen arousal state.

In addition, to the extent that you can control the environment in which you place yourself, you can control the stimuli that affect your arousal. An aware person can choose environmental stimuli that will affect his arousal in a desired way and avoid those that could push his arousal to un-wanted levels. With these perspectives in mind, let's explore the world of perception.

EXPECTATIONS

Your body consults your mental images to predict and prepare for physiological needs before they arise. The anticipation of danger, for example, puts your body in an aroused state, ready for bursts of energy. The expectation of activity increases breathing and heart rate. Processes like visualization and the Carpenter Effect (see the Mental Training section of chapter 4) serve to make the body more capable of performing in scenarios you expect and think about frequently. Using inner thoughts as a model of what to expect, the mind sets about preparing the body for their eventual occurrence.

In this way, a part of you unconsciously moves toward your dominant expectations. Expect success on a route and your mind plans for the moves you anticipate making. If you're dynoing for a hold, it plans the

positions you'll be in and how your body will react once you catch it; while lunging, for example, you prepare for the finger positions the next hold will require. These measures make you more likely to succeed because your body is readied before the move is completed. Since you expected to continue, your mind already knows how to react once you're there. And since positive expectations are less threatening, arousal

Jibé Tribout lunging with conviction on the committing last move of Miss Catastrophe.

levels are not pushed to counterproductive levels.

Expect failure and your body stiffens to brace for a fall. Your mind plans for the positions and path a fall might take, and even prepares excuses for fellow climbing partners before you fall.

With negative expectations, your thoughts can contribute to your own downfall. When Bruno dynos without conviction, he sometimes just taps the hold he was going for with his hand to suggest that he "almost" did it. But the uncommitted gesture of the hand gives away his expectation of failure.

By filling your mind with images of the experience of failure, negative thoughts like these take the place of attention that could have been devoted to progressing onward. Since these mental pictures constitute a perceived future, part of you cannot help but prepare for them. These preparations for failure poison your efforts. And since negative expectations are typically accompanied by a perception of threat, they often push the body to a level of arousal above that optimal for climbing. So although expectations are little more than guesses,

they become self-fulfilling prophecies. For this reason, how you deal with your expectations is important.

We'll look at two basic approaches to reducing the effects of negative expectations on your climbing. One involves taking steps to reduce the role of anticipation in your performance. By freeing your mind of the limits that expectations impose, you climb with an open mind and are best able to express your potential. First, however, we'll look at ways of making the expectations you do have into the kind that work *for* you rather than against you.

These two approaches may seem contradictory at first. They're not. Together they aim to reduce the number and intensity of expectations crowding your mind and ensure that the expectations you do harbor are positive ones. When successful, these steps result in an open mind founded on a background of positive expectations.

Promote Positive Expectations

In any situation, some factors favor success while others point toward failure. Because of

---

Max's Reasons to Succeed on Ruthless Redpoint

- My other hardest routes have been on this same type of rock.
- I've been training more this season, so I'm ready for a breakthrough.
- The weather and conditions are right for this route at this time of year.
- I've been doing "worked" boulder problems, so I'm better at remembering sequences this season.
- I've done my training and "paid my dues," so it makes sense that I will climb better than I ever have.
- My new rope will be light and frictionless against the rock.

Max's Yeah-but's Converted to Positive Statements

- ("Yeah, but this would be the hardest route I've ever done!")
  The routes I've done this spring have made me ready for the hardest route I've ever done.
- ("Yeah, but I'm bad at dynos and this route is rumored to have some on it!")
  What I lack in dyno ability I make up for with my lock-off strength. Plus I've been working on my dynos, so they'll be better than they've ever been before.
- ("Yeah, but people will think I'm lame if I don't eventually redpoint it.")
  People think I'm bad at worked routes as it is. Their lack of expectations takes the pressure off me. I can only come out ahead.

the self-fulfilling quality of expectations, it's important to expect the best from yourself, to be optimistic, and to climb with conviction. Focusing on the factors that bode well for you helps you do this. If you suspect that negative expectations hinder your climbing, try the following exercise.

Explore the reasons why you expect to succeed. Review the preparations you've made and the experiences you've had that qualify you to realize your current undertaking. Remind yourself of any other factors that point toward success.

As you are making this list, your mind will probably respond with "Yeah, but . . ." statements. Go over each "yeah-but" in your mind and either convert it into something positive or dismiss it altogether. Some people write these things down, as Max did in these examples.

Practicing success through mental training (see chapter 4) will also help you reduce negative expectations. The repetitive images of success mental training gives you are models of success for your body to follow.

Reduce the Role of Expectations

Success is more difficult when it's not okay to fail. Expectations plague us most in situations where outcomes are questionable and vital. They fill our minds when a lot hinges on success or failure. By contrast, when we're not threatened the need to predict and

Max's Reasons Why It's Okay to Not Succeed on *Ruthless Redpoint*

- I'll still have my girlfriend, Ruth.
- I'll still have my $500 savings for my road trip next month.
- I'll still have the rest of the summer to climb.
- What I'll learn by working an overhanging route is worth it whether I succeed or fail.

prepare for the possible outcomes of our activities is reduced

Although you can't eliminate expectations altogether, you can diminish their role in your performances by reducing their threat. If, in your own mind, you decrease the magnitude of what hangs in the balance, you can reduce your need to anticipate outcomes.

Reduce the gravity of the situation. Put aside why you need to succeed, and dwell on reasons why it's all right to fail at your undertaking. Remember the positive aspects of your life that will remain unchanged if the outcome of the effort in question is not what you would like. This will help you keep the weight of the task in realistic proportion with the rest of your life. Also consider things that will make the experience worthwhile regardless of its outcome.

These exercises serve to decrease the importance of the possible outcomes in your mind. By reducing the weight of the situation, they lower your need to predict and prepare for its end result.

You can also help to reduce the role of expectations by getting deeply absorbed in the activity mentally. Recall the first time you tried to ride a bike. You weren't trying to predict what would happen. You were immersed in the newness flooding your senses. You were free of expectations. Climbing can offer the same flood of newness, even after years of doing it, if you can let yourself be engrossed by what your experiences are telling you. Expectations become irrelevant. Your mind opens. And your mental energies are freed from comparisons to imagined outcomes.

This requires a deep knowledge that you are safe and that all possible outcomes are okay. When this is your perspective (and when it's true), climbing is valuable regardless of the outcome. Participation becomes the central objective, for it is the sole path to both improvement and pleasure. Its course is cobbled with the inseparable partners success and failure, and it is the only path to the satisfactions of climbing.

SELF-IMAGE

One thing your predicting and preparing mechanism consults in forming its expectations is your self-image. If you think you're a lame climber, your expectations will be lower than if you think you've got secret talent waiting to be manifested.

A detailed study of how to improve self-image is beyond the scope of a book on climbing. But realize that self-image will affect your climbing. For now, some basic guidelines will help you avoid being your own worst enemy.

- Reward your successes but don't punish yourself for failing to meet your expectations. Failure is not a cause for frustration, and hating yourself for failing will not make you a better climber. More about failure in a moment.

- Take care of your ego through the ups and downs of climbing. Putting others down or talking big to boost your self-esteem is a dead-end way to keep your ego satisfied, because even if you succeed in fooling others, you don't fool yourself. Your opinion of yourself has more direct effect on your performance than others' opinions of you.

- Take a broad view of your climbing accomplishments rather than relying on receiving positive feedback from your climbing every time you go out. Experienced athletes don't stop having bad days; they accept themselves and don't have to psychologically recover from bad days as do their less developed peers.

Positive expectations and self-image will not make a world-class athlete out of a beginner. Rather, they are factors that tip the scales for many climbers when an undertaking hovers at the boundaries of their limitations. The fact that they are psychologically rooted doesn't mean you can change them at will. Like any other skill, changing your perceptions takes attention and work for an extended period of time.

MOTIVATION

Since motivation involves effort applied in a direction, all motivation has some kind of orientation. You can orient your motivation around obtaining pleasure, avoiding pain, accumulating money, or many other factors. Even people involved in the same activity have very different orientations to their motivations. Because of the interdependence of psychological, autonomic, and motor processes, motivational orientation has direct consequences for performance.

An important aspect of climbing motivation involves its orientation with respect to success and failure. The difference between the two perspectives discussed below is purely perceptual, but the effects on climbing performance are dramatic and concrete.

Success Versus Failure Orientation

Failure-oriented athletes fear failure and try to *not* do whatever it entails. They are motivated to avoid making fools out of themselves and to avoid failure's consequences. They regard failures as important reflections of their own worth. The internal dialogues of this state give it away: "Just don't blow it; stop shaking; don't get the wrong hand sequence."

The problems with failure orientation are twofold. First, it lacks direction. Orienting your motivation around what you want to move away from doesn't direct you *toward* anything. The mind's preparing and predicting mechanism, which guides the arousal level, has only undesired scenarios to predict and prepare for. Attempts to avoid mistakes associated with failure thus provide no target, no mental model for success. Second, failure orientation is a fundamentally threatened way of viewing the world. As a result it produces excessive arousal levels, lowering coordination and impairing technique.

In many athletes, their consistent failure orientation becomes a failure expectation. When failure occurs, they consider themselves responsible for failing. But when they're successful, they credit luck, conditions, or other external factors.

In a failure-oriented outlook, failing and not failing are the only possible outcomes.

Success-oriented people are motivated by achievement. They expect success and direct their efforts to reap the rewards it brings. The existence and threat of failure neither propels nor hinders them; it is simply less pertinent in their motivation. Such people consider failures irrelevant as statements about themselves. Their successes define them, not their failures.

Their internal dialogues sound different: "Crank it out; steady with the legs; sequence it right." These are positive statements of goals toward which they strive. They view success as their own personal achievement, having little to do with luck or outside factors. They even have a hard time taking responsibility for failure; they blame the conditions, bad luck, or spectators when things go badly.

The expectation of success is one source of the "go-for-it" conviction that character-

izes top performances. A climber who dynos with conviction will latch holds he could never manage if he expected failure on the same move.

No one thinks exclusively one way or the other all the time. But it's not by chance that world-class athletes perform mostly with the latter orientation. Success orientation promotes better movement by improving the climber's emotional and mental environment. Stating a positive goal offers a mental model of success for which the body can anticipate and prepare. In addition, since they consider success to be more meaningful than failure, success-oriented climbers have little to lose. A success-oriented athlete either succeeds or doesn't succeed; she either wins something or doesn't win something. In neither case is there a loss. This reduces the threat involved in any undertaking. Since they're less threatened by challenges, success-oriented athletes more easily achieve the lower arousal levels optimal for technique-dependent activities like climbing.

Developing Success-Oriented Motivation

In some people, a consistent failure orientation is rooted in psychological phenomena beyond the scope of this book. But simple aspects of how you go about pursuing what you want in climbing significantly affect your orientation.

A careful program of goal setting orients your plans, actions, and accomplishments around what you want to achieve. By focusing your attention and efforts on chosen goals, it instills a habit of success-oriented motivation.

Effective goal setting is neither quick nor simple. For it to work, great care must be taken in choosing your goals. Without such care, goal setting can work against you.

1. For goals to work, they must be stated positively. By framing goals in terms of what you want (more endurance, for example) rather than what you're trying to avoid (falling off), you create a mental image of something to work toward. Negatively phrased goals provide no image of what you're striving for. You can't move toward the reverse of an idea.

2. Goals should be set in such a way that you know when you've achieved them. Stating "I want much greater lock-off strength" is a nonattainable goal, for you never know when you've achieved it.

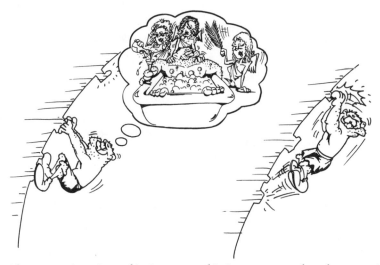

With success orientation, achieving or not achieving success are the only two possibilities. In neither outcome is there a failure.

Saying "I want to be able to lock every move on the first pitch of *Schwarzenegger"* is an attainable goal.

3. You need intermediate steps to mark your progress toward any goal that will take you more than a few months to achieve. Successfully achieved intermediate goals let you know you're on the right track and rejuvenate your motivation toward your longer-term goals. Failure at intermediate goals warns that your current methods aren't working, preventing further use of them.

4. Goals must be realistic. Success at current goals fuels motivation toward future goals, so it's important that you actually achieve a good proportion of your goals. Psychologists claim motivation is strongest when you have a fifty-fifty chance of achieving your aim. Goals should thus be high enough to motivate you and to demand your best effort, yet low enough that they are achievable much of the time.

5. What we become is a result of the little things we do on a day-to-day basis. Having goals helps us achieve our ends because they remind us of where we intend to go and thereby direct what we do with our time. The more consistently aware of our goals we are, the more likely we are to do the things necessary to achieve them. Lots of things can be done to maintain this awareness of your goals. Writing them down is the simplest and most effective of these. Review them periodically, so that you always know what they are when you're training.

Of equal importance to these general guidelines are the particulars of your situation. Your goals must reflect your own unique characteristics, resources, and motivations. You must weave a consideration of the following factors into your goal setting:

- Your limiting abilities and skills
- The training volume you can handle and your recovery rate
- Your current state of fitness
- The crags and facilities available to you
- The principles of climbing and training.

Success-oriented people have not been mysteriously spared the agony of defeat. They just don't agonize over it. To a large extent, your orientation reflects what you consider most revealing about you as a person and how you go about pursuing what you want in your life. Dwell on the rewards of success, not the penalty of failure. From a success orientation you create the best psychological environment for climbing.

Frustration and Failure

Dealing with frustration as a climber has to do with perceiving the nature of the sport. The art of climbing can be frustrating if you're unaware or unaccepting of its realities. But if you realize and accept its characteristics, there's little to be frustrated

about. Again, only perceptual differences separate these two views.

If, for example, you expect to climb better each and every week you go climbing, you're ignoring the reality of athletic progress. When you accept the nature of climbing, and the fact that bad days or weeks will occur no matter what your climbing level, it is much less discouraging.

Consider an experience many find frustrating. You link a route from bottom to top with a top-rope, then expect that you can redpoint it on your next try, but you fail to do so. The world hasn't done you an injustice. You simply failed to account for some aspect of the extent to which top-roping a route translates into the ability to redpoint it. If you're willing to get past the emotions this brings up, you can find out the specific nature of your error and learn how to keep from making it in the future.

Perhaps you didn't take into account that fear would reduce your fluidity on lead. Maybe you didn't consider that you'd have to hold on to some holds for longer in order to make the clips. Maybe you needed different sequences to allow you to clip in on lead. Whether you're conscious of your errors or not, you were ultimately responsible. Awareness of your errors is 90 percent of what it takes to change. Anger only blinds you to the lessons failure offers. You won't stop footholds from being difficult to stand on, distractions from pulling at your attention, or chance things from occurring. But you can increase your ability to deal with all these factors.

Feeling miserable about your failures only haunts your future efforts with the ghosts of bad experiences past. Nor is it enough to simply ignore or brush off your failures. You must welcome them (if only grudgingly) as vital corrections to your estimations of what you need and what you have.

If you're willing to look at them, failures point out the weaknesses you have more bluntly and directly than any other part of your climbing. Make peace with your failures. To really progress, you must embrace them as you do your successes. They are worthy and necessary associates. By missing out on the benefits of failure, those who avoid their risks and pains only cultivate long-term stagnation—the one kind of failure worth actively avoiding.

Realize why you climb. Climbing is not rewarding in spite of its frustrations. It is rewarding *because* of the very factors that can make it frustrating. The beautiful complexity that makes it possible to sometimes fail when you expected to succeed, and to succeed when you expected to fail, renders mastery at any level at once elusive and priceless.

7. BEHAVIORAL APPROACHES TO PSYCHOLOGICAL CONTROL

Next time you get agitated in traffic or frustrated with someone, try a simple experiment. Take a moment to relax the muscles in your jaw, face, and shoulders, and take a deep breath, exhaling slowly.

You'll find that not only does your body calm down, but your racing thoughts do too. This shows how changing one of the processes of the inner triad affects the others: the breathing and facial changes counteract some symptoms of autonomic arousal. But they affect psychological (and motor) processes as well.

The behavioral approach to psychological control is founded on this interconnectedness of the three inner processes. We will look at ways of responding to your environment and specific techniques that can bring about changes in the inner triad processes. Through practice at such exercises, you can develop control over your state of arousal and learn to adapt it to suit your specific needs for different climbing activities.

Don't fall for the popular misconception that once you understand them, using psychological techniques is simply a matter of "doing it." The exercises that follow can't rescue you from psychological disasters until you've practiced them extensively and learned their subtleties.

Since we acquire our psychological habits over the course of our lives, counterproductive psychological patterns don't die easily. Preferred patterns must be practiced over and over before they come naturally.

Bruno uses psychological techniques.

Psychological training thus requires the same effort and patience as physical training. Because the results of psychological training are hard to measure, it takes discipline to do it with dedication. But with directed effort real changes can be made, and destructive patterns can be replaced with constructive ones. If you decide any of the techniques described are for you, start working with them now.

Remember that although the exercises given below will affect your performance state, they are not the solution to all your psychological troubles. Elements outside the sports realm contribute to your psychological state too. For example, if you're plagued while climbing by a gnawing feeling that you're running out of money or about to get fired from your job, it's best to deal with these issues directly. The exercises below can help you make the best of this kind of psychological backdrop, but they certainly won't change it.

ADJUSTING AROUSAL THROUGH THE INNER TRIAD

We've discussed how a change in psychological, autonomic, or motor processes influences the whole inner triad. The methods that follow work on one or more

Long fall on a bolt-on route at the Gruga-Halle in Essen, Germany.

processes to affect overall arousal and are grouped according to their approach. Some will target arousal symptoms from one process exclusively; others are more holistic, aiming to alter several types of arousal symptoms at once. If you find them effective, or feel that psychological phenomena are central in your climbing performance, we encourage you to do further reading for more detailed information.

Since success hinges on accurately targeting the problem, use the weakest link principle to choose the most important methods for you personally. Ask yourself if the symptoms of high arousal affect you most in psychological, autonomic, or motor processes. If one stands out, targeting the area in which your worst symptoms lie will produce the greatest results.

Techniques Aimed at Psychological Processes

The techniques described below aim to calm the psychological part of your inner triad. They focus on the mind and work to change the way your thoughts and feelings play out as you climb.

Progressive Desensitization

Just as kids get desensitized to violence by watching it on television, you can habituate yourself to many of the troubling psychological aspects of climbing.

Many climbers try to avoid thinking about things that intimidate them, such as falling, because they worry that dwelling on their fears will amplify them. "If I keep putting it out of my mind," Bruno reasons, "maybe it'll stop coming back."

But psychologists suggest that we don't get over troubling thoughts and emotions by suppressing them. The experiences that trouble us are simply too much to handle. To desensitize ourselves to them we must gradually reduce their emotional potency by exposing ourselves to less threatening versions of them.

For example, Julia wants to redpoint the *Slicer,* a beautiful but intimidating overhanging arete. At 5.10d, it would be one of her hardest ascents, but she simply cannot imagine herself doing it—she jerks awake from nightmares in which she's climbing it.

To use progressive desensitization Julia begins by rating her fear on a scale of one to ten. Julia rates leading the *Slicer* as an eight on her fear scale. Top-roping it is a seven because of the frightening swings between the sparse bolts. Next, Julia decides which of the climbs she is capable of doing intimidate her the most. She then rates those on her fear scale.

She decides that top-roping *Cat in the Hat Arete* is a three; leading it is a four. She's willing to lead *Cat in the Hat* if she top-ropes it first, but that still leaves her several points below top-roping the *Slicer.* To bridge this gap, Julia must find routes of an intermediate fear factor.

Progressive desensitization involves gradually exposing yourself to more intimidating situations in order to reach a goal that may initially seem inconceivable. By using a progressive approach to aretes that intimidate her, Julia gradually lowers her intimidation of the *Slicer.* When she finally redpointed her nemesis four months later, Julia rated it a calm four on her enhanced fear scale. Now she has her sights set on *Bloodbath.* . . .

Reality Replacement

Bad choices and poor performances from our past sometimes haunt us long after they occur because they replay in our minds. When we can't let go of such experiences, we end up mentally rehearsing them over and over. As a result, our performance suffers when we encounter similar circumstances.

Originally used by native Americans, reality replacement is a useful technique for overcoming such problems. It involves revisualizing negative experiences of the past and substituting a desired behavior or response for an undesired one you made.

Max's foot once slipped from a small edge in a competition, and he fell on what should have been easy climbing. He had a hard time forgiving himself for it, and he couldn't stop reviewing it in his mind. After that mishap, Max got the jitters every time he had to stand on a small foothold in a competition.

On learning of the reality replacement technique, Max used two different reality replacements for his bad memory. Following the guidelines for mental training (see chapter 4), he relaxed in his easy chair, calmed his body, and began revisualizing the incident. He imagined himself starting up the competition route in lifelike detail. When he came to where his foot slipped, he vividly pictured a new sequence of events. He experienced his foot slipping, but his body reacted quickly, and he held on. Regaining his composure, he climbed the rest of the route.

In his second reality replacement, Max

pictured himself eyeing the small edge before placing his foot on it. Seeing that it was small and anticipating the precision it would take to stand on it, he placed his foot carefully as he stood up on it. He used the foothold with a constant moderate pressure, and even as he moved off it, he was careful not to put any sudden thrusts on that foot. Moving onward, he finished the route.

Once you've established your replacement reality, you must repeat it many times to erase the negative associations you connect with that situation and replace them with positive associations.

Concentration

Many climbers have concentration problems. At the moments when they most need to focus on the moves before them, they'll mentally wander to what their belayer is up to, what the climber next to them is doing, or seemingly random thoughts. Numerous exercises exist for improving your concentration. We've found this one useful.

Take a comfortable seated position and close your eyes. Begin slow, deep, and quiet breathing (see below), and turn

Concentration.

your attention inward. When you're ready, begin counting each of your exhalations, starting with one. When you reach ten, start with one again. If you lose your place or fail to stop at ten, trace back the thought that distracted you. Notice how, why, and when the thought started. Then resume counting.

If you repeat this exercise for ten-minute stretches, you'll notice improvement in the focus of your attention and the quality of your awareness. If you can't stay awake, you may need sleep more than this exercise. But your concentration will sharpen and resist drowsiness with practice.

Techniques Aimed at Autonomic Processes

The autonomic system operates in the background, quietly adjusting and maintaining what we normally regard as our involuntary body functions. But though its workings are inaccessible to normal acts of will, the autonomic system is reachable by indirect means. Let's look at a few.

Breathing

Breath stands at the gateway to the autonomic system. It is the only body function you can control both consciously and unconsciously, because two independent sets of nerves (one voluntary, the other autonomic) regulate it.

It is not by chance that many meditation systems use breath as their central focus. Harvard M.D. Andrew Weil calls breathing "the bridge between mind and body, the connection between consciousness and unconsciousness," and "the master key to health and wellness, a function we can learn to regulate and develop in order to improve our physical, mental, and spiritual well-being."

Breathing is especially important in our sport. Climbers flirt constantly with the threat of a downward plummet, and as they catch themselves from such mistakes, they also catch their breath. Out of fear and anxiety climbers often use shallow, rapid, and irregular breathing. In addition, a climber's movements and positions sometimes require a complete suspension of breathing: when core muscles are loaded to more than half their maximum strength, breathing is not possible. No wonder most climbers don't know how to breathe.

It is difficult to remain calm when your breathing is shallow or irregular. Likewise it is hard to be highly aroused when your breathing is smooth, deep, and quiet. By breathing in a manner characteristic of high arousal, too many climbers cultivate other symptoms of anxiety. Although you may not be able to access your arousal state directly, you can choose the quality of your breathing, and the effects on your arousal will be dramatic.

Because of the importance of breath, climbers have a lot to gain by learning to breathe effectively whenever they can and to resume fluid breathing immediately after any necessary interruption.

Exercise 1: First, get to know what full, effective breathing feels like by developing the ability to breath smoothly, deeply, and quietly. Take a minute, close your eyes, and see how smooth, deep, and quiet you can make your breathing. Notice how even between inhaling and exhaling, your breathing never really stops, since there are no two consecutive instants during which you're at the same point in the breath cycle.

Once you know how SDQ (smooth, deep, and quiet) breathing feels, try it several times a day. With practice, you'll be able to switch to it quickly.

Exercise 2: In climbing, SDQ breathing is not always possible. It's essential, then, that climbers be skilled at shifting from halted breathing back to SDQ breathing immediately.

Try this first in ideal conditions. Sit back in a chair, close your eyes, and begin SDQ breathing. Next, picture a powerful move on a climb you know. As you execute it in your mind, hold your breath as you would from the effort it takes you. Once you've completed the move, resume SDQ breathing. Repeat the transition from interrupted breathing to SDQ breathing until you can make the switch immediately.

In addition to bringing this into your climbing, you can also practice it in other parts of your life, resuming SDQ breathing immediately after a near miss in traffic or a startling scene in a movie.

The Quieting Reflex

Where other techniques are normally done as "homework," the quieting reflex (QR) stands apart as a technique aimed at the "scene of the crime" of stress. The procedure takes only a few seconds and can be done whenever stimuli from your environment trigger a stress response. It is one of the most powerful exercises listed here for reducing arousal.

QR aims to prevent arousal *as it starts* through a competing hierarchy of responses incompatible with the first several seconds of the body's typical fight-or-flight response. By intercepting stressors, it nips the symptoms of high arousal in the bud. Because of its brevity, many athletes too impatient for some of the other psychological techniques find the time for QR.

To use QR, you must first have enough awareness to realize when something in your environment has triggered an escalation in your arousal. Take note when you swear silently to yourself, catch your breath, or tighten up your body in response to a slip while climbing. On recognizing stress, QR consists of a three-step response:

1. Smile to yourself inwardly with your eyes and mouth.
2. Take a slow, deep abdominal breath and make your breathing flow.
3. Then exhale through your mouth, letting your jaw, tongue, and shoulders go limp.

You're best off learning QR in low-stress situations, where you can take the extra time to practice these steps. But after a few months, QR becomes a reflex, hard-wired into your natural way of dealing with the stimuli around you. This reflex serves climbers well because it takes only seconds to perform and it operates "behind the scenes," kicking into effect even as you continue other activities. Because it's easy to employ, variations of QR are used by many top climbers before, during, and after a challenging route.

Biofeedback

Many physiological processes normally under autonomic control can be brought under conscious control and influenced by act of will. Biofeedback involves monitoring physiological functions normally ignored in day-to-day life. It is a skill climbers can apply to control their state of arousal.

One readily available type of biofeedback device monitors galvanic skin response (GSR), producing a tone that goes up or down in response to how moist your finger skin is. GSR units sell for under $15 at many electronics stores. GSR biofeedback has special relevance to climbing, because sweaty skin sacrifices finger friction. With the growth in the popularity of running, heart rate monitors have also become more widely available.

If you try biofeedback on your own, notice how different thoughts affect your biofeedback signal. When you begin to feel you can influence it, try intentionally thinking of something that heightens your arousal. Visualize an intimidating climb, and once you feel involved in the images, come back to your feedback signal. How's it doing?

If there's a significant change, note how great its effect is, then experiment with techniques described here to lower the biofeedback signal. Aim to be able to drop it quickly when it is raised by unsettling thoughts. Eventually you can learn to exercise the acts of will that keep the signal down while conversing, doing vivid imagery, or concentrating intently on something.

A Technique Aimed at Motor Processes

High arousal shows itself in more than just your involuntary systems. Throughout your body, your motor system reflects high arousal through partial contractions of selected muscles ("grim" facial expressions, tight shoulders) and increased muscle tone throughout the body. The following technique works to reduce the effects of arousal in the muscular system. Since many climbers are more body-oriented than less athletic people, they often find its effects more dramatic than those of techniques focused on purely mental phenomena.

Progressive Muscle Relaxation

Muscles maintain a certain minimum tension even at rest through an alternating contraction of a small percentage of fibers. In states of high arousal, this percentage is higher, and the tightness this causes consumes extra energy, disrupts fluid body movement, and reduces the amount of blood that can flow through a muscle when it's "relaxed."

Although research has shown that people can reduce the state of resting tension within muscles by act of will alone, the effects are more dramatic and longer lasting when an intense contraction precedes the relaxation. This combination of contraction and relaxation is the foundation of progressive muscle relaxation.

To use the technique, take a comfortable seated position or lie on your back. Relax, and breathe smoothly and deeply, feeling the weight of your body against the surface supporting you. Close your eyes and move your focus from the outer world into your body.

Focus on one hand and close it to a fist. Squeeze it tighter and tighter, reaching maximum contraction after a couple seconds. Concentrate on the feeling of tension throughout the hand and forearm. After holding it for three to five seconds, release the tension suddenly and completely. It may feel as if it takes a few seconds to let go of all muscle tension. Relax for several seconds, feeling the relaxation sweep into that area. Then repeat the process with the other hand. Maintain the state of relaxation in each area you've relaxed as you continue with other parts of your body.

Next make sure there's at least a partial bend at the elbow, and contract the biceps and other muscles of one upper arm. Feel the tension, then suddenly relax, as before. Enjoy the feeling of relaxation for a few moments before moving to the other arm.

Continue this process by working down your body, first contracting, then relaxing. Carry on with your forehead and face, neck and shoulders, stomach, legs, feet, and so on.

Some athletes find the technique too relaxing to use before practicing their sports. But with relaxed muscles, your body is in a better state for recovery after climbing and on rest days. Most important, learning how to relax muscles at will can help you *while* you climb. By completely relaxing your muscles at shake-outs on a route, or during the brief moments between gripping one hold and the next, you contract fewer muscle fibers at rest and increase your recovery anytime a hand is not weighted.

BEHAVIORAL CHOICES

While the preceding techniques can significantly affect performance state, many simple decisions we make or fail to make also affect our arousal. Although some people choose to ignore their effects, we cannot escape their influences.

Music

Sounds directly affect our state of arousal. We're so constantly surrounded by many of them that we often forget this. But just think what a horror movie would be like accompanied by Disney music.

If there's music playing while you climb, notice its effects. Think about whether they're desirable or not, and do what you can to choose what you let inside you, just as you choose the more tangible types of nutrition you consume.

Since fast-paced music often pushes arousal upward, for example, it can be helpful in powerful bouldering sessions, where the strength benefits of higher arousal are a plus. But using the same types of music as you prepare for and attempt a tricky on-sight can hinder you by taking your arousal above the level necessary for technical precision.

Peer Pressure

Peer pressure is a strong agent of arousal for many climbers. If you recognize this, you can use it to your advantage by choosing when you want to expose yourself to peer pressure and when you're best off avoiding it.

For example, bouldering enthusiasts sometimes use techniques to amplify peer pressure, taking advantage of the strength gains that result. When Max feels under-aroused, he'll bet his partners a snack that he can do a boulder problem on his next try or within a certain amount of time. The pressure this adds is often all it takes to get him repsyched and rearoused to the extent he needs to perform optimally.

CONCLUSIONS

Obviously, many other techniques for psychological regulation exist. We have provided a sampling of those that have proven most useful in the situations climbers encounter.

Remember, no performance state is universally optimal. Each state sacrifices some qualities for the benefit of others (see the diagram on the effects of arousal on motor processes in chapter 5). To use good "psychological technique" you must continually reconsider your needs, reevaluate your state, and choose methods of adjusting your arousal appropriately. Developing skill in psycho-regulation takes much practice.

But don't despair over the difficulty of achieving climbing's ideal performance state. Activities with straightforward psychological components like walking, running, and eating cannot challenge us in the same way. They lack mental intricacy. The ongoing tension between the responses our instincts pull us toward and the responses we can create through a careful process of intention is one source of climbing's intrigue.

8. PHYSICAL TRAINING PRINCIPLES

This chapter offers introductory guidelines for the chapters that follow. These principles apply to physical training in general and are as important as the specifics of training outlined later in the book. Bring them into your climbing and you'll make the science of training into an art.

TRAINING ADAPTATION AND IMPROVEMENT

All life forms adapt as best they can to the environment and conditions they live in. When conditions are unchanging, most organisms operate in a steady state of equilibrium, or homeostasis. Their bodies are essentially unchanged from one month to the next, because the *catabolic* processes involving the breakdown of tissues and the expenditure of energy are balanced with *anabolic* processes that reconstruct tissues,

assimilate new materials, and replenish energy stores.

Physical training works by disrupting this equilibrium. A training session is a controlled catabolic stimulus that stresses muscles, bones, and connective tissues and depletes energy stores. By the end of a workout, performance ability drops below the normal equilibrium level. In recovering from the training session, the body tries to adapt to a lifestyle that includes this training routine. It thus recovers beyond its former state and in athletic lingo, "supercompensates" for the catabolic workout.

Supercompensation results from adaptations that make the body better able to handle the stress that the workout imposed. Chemical adaptations to training include more enzymes and cellular energy converters to kindle chemical reactions, greater storage of glycogen and other fuels, and

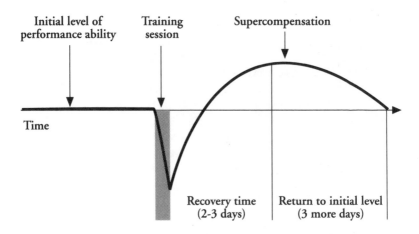

Initial level of performance ability | Training session | Supercompensation

Time

Recovery time (2-3 days) | Return to initial level (3 more days)

Supercompensation after a training session.

lactic acid neutralizers in the bloodstream. Muscles get bigger, tendons get stronger, blood vessels grow and proliferate. Even the nervous and hormonal systems make adaptive changes to the stress of training.

Training Volume

Improvement and regression hinge on the *balance* of catabolic and anabolic activity. If either is insufficient, progress will be sacrificed. If catabolic volume is too low, your training may not be providing enough stimulus to cause supercompensation. When too high, it can overwhelm your ability to recover.

There are four components of training volume: quantity, intensity, density, and frequency.

Quantity

Clearly, the more you work out, the more stress you give your body to recover from. If you're used to climbing three or four routes on a climbing day and you do seven or eight instead, you've doubled your quantity, and you'll need more recovery time.

Intensity

You could also increase your training volume without doing more routes. If the routes you choose are harder and take greater effort, you raise your training volume through increased intensity. Technically, intensity refers to the load on the muscles and the percentage of your maximum strength required.

Density

Consider a workout that normally takes you an hour to do. If you squeeze it into a thirty-five-minute period by shortening rests or other inactive periods, you increase your training volume by raising your training density.

Frequency

Frequency refers to how often you work out and the length of time between workouts. If each workout is done during the period of supercompensation from your last workout (two or three days later), the affected systems of the body recover and supercompensate before being subjected to another training session (see top figure, page 88). You thus progress to steadily higher levels of ability.

If workouts are done too frequently, however, the body will not have had time to recover from the last workout before the next one takes place. As a result the climber gets weaker with each successive training session, as shown in the bottom figure on page 88.

For improvement to continue in the long term, training volume must increase at a pace the body can keep up with. In this way, the body constantly adapts to ever higher levels of training stimulus. A volume that was once a sufficient stimulus for improvement may only *maintain* performance at a higher level of ability. If training volume goes unchanged, the body plateaus at the new level.

Volume, Fatigue, and Regeneration

The sensation of fatigue is partly a protective mechanism. By making further work unpleasant, it prevents your body from depleting its reserves to levels from which it cannot recover.

There are two basic types of fatigue. *Local fatigue* affects the local areas directly

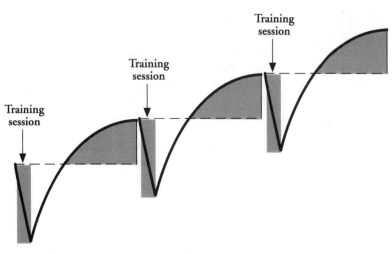

Improvement from successive workouts.

involved in a sport. It can be caused by microtrauma in the muscles, the accumulation of wastes like lactic acid, or the depletion of glycogen, proteins, electrolytes, and so forth within the muscles. Local fatigue is evident in the soreness, tight muscles, cramps, and weakness that can follow intense physical exertion. Deep local fatigue is acceptable, even desirable in some types of physical training.

Central fatigue involves the nervous and hormonal systems that support recovery

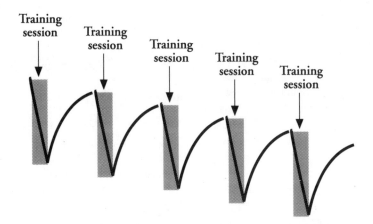

Regression due to insufficient recovery time.

Climbers on a 5.6 tower in the Bielatal region of Saxony, Germany. Strict ethics at Saxony permit only soft protection (webbing or rope knots), ground-up ascents, and no chalk.

Cathy Beloeil redpointing The Gift 5.12c/d at Red Rocks, outside of Las Vegas.

Udo Neumann on Smith Rocks' Chain Reaction.

Dale Goddard on his Hueco V10, Serves You Right.

Marc LeMenestrel climbing Le Privilege du Serpent *(7c+) on-sight at France's futuristic crag, Ceuse.*

Bernd Arnold climbing Hasenherz *(5.12), at the sport's birthplace, and the world's largest climbing area, Saxony, Germany. Bernd Arnold has set climbing standards there for the last three decades. Inset: Jerry Moffat making his historic ascent of* Papy on Sight 7c+, *spring 1984, Verdon Gorge, France.*

Dale Goddard and April Walters on a 5.10+ in Smith Rocks' Cocaine Gully.

Amy Irvine on Little Cottonwood Canyon's All Chalk No Action, 5.11d, Salt Lake, Utah.

Dale Goddard on Scarface, 5.14a, at Smith Rocks, Oregon.

Master boulderer of Fontainbleau, Jacky Godoffe, on L'Abbé Resina *(7c)*

Icelandic hopeful Dominique Gudmundsdottir bouldering at Cabo San Lucas, South Baja, Mexico.

Mike Paul climbing the well-known Joshua Tree boulder problem, Stem Gem *(B1), backward.*

Udo Neumann, high over France's Verdon River on Wide Is Love *5.9. Inset: Isabelle Patissier competing in the 1991 World Championships in Frankfurt.*

Boone Speed powering the American Fork testpiece Blow of Death *(a.k.a.* Dead Souls*) 5.13d.*

Geoff Weigand on the Mushroom Roof in Hueco Tanks, Texas.

Dale Goddard on Ramora *at the City of Rocks, Idaho.*

Martin Yoisten on The Minnow, *5.10, at the City of Rocks, Idaho.*

Jibé Tribout attempting
Miss Catastrophe. *8c+,*
Buoux, France.

Dale Goddard on The Prowser. *Little*
Cottonwood Canyon, Utah.

Bobbie Bensman on Vulcan Crawl, *Logan, Utah.*

*Francois Dreyfus
on* Agincourt,
Buoux, France.

Smith Rocks' Monkey Face, with climbers on Space Monkey *and* Just Do It.

Dale Goddard attempting Just Do It.

Mike Beck starting up Just Do It.

Jibé Tribout working an 8c+ project at Orgon, France.

Gina Sorensen on Aards on Promenade, *Big Cottonwood, Utah.*

Jibé Tribout and François Legrand climbing in the Calanques, France.

throughout the body. Central fatigue results from the cumulative burden of local fatigue throughout the body. Exhausting the body with a deep central fatigue sacrifices local recovery and is undesirable for climbers. The signs of central fatigue are decreased concentration, slower reaction time, and decreased precision of movements.

For most athletes, a simple layoff from the activity (passive recovery) leads to recuperation from local and central fatigue. For climbers who demand the most from their bodies, certain exercises can quicken the recovery process (see chapter 11, General Endurance).

The recovery times for most training exercises are given in this book. These times are for an intermediate climber; recovery times for advanced climbers may be somewhat shorter, while those for beginners can be longer.

Diminishing Returns

The ability to physically improve is not unlimited. We all have our own personal limitations, defined by genetic factors like muscle fiber proportions, strength of immune functioning, body type, and other influences. The closer you get to your genetic limits, the more difficult it becomes to make further physical improvements. For someone who's never climbed before, the addition of almost any kind of climbing activity can enhance performance. But for someone who has climbed for several years, her ability represents her adaptations to the volume of training she normally has time to do. If she reduces that volume, she may regress.

To reap great physical improvement as a beginner is thus no piece of art. But to improve after years of climbing and training takes careful attention to the quantity, quality, and variety of an athlete's training, along with awareness and care in avoiding injuries. The more advanced your ability, the more you flirt with the dangers of overtraining and the harder you must work for smaller and smaller increments of gain.

Having said this, however, it's important to realize that the plateaus athletes reach are rarely the result of genetic limits. Most athletes sabotage their efforts to approach their potential through mistargeted training priorities, inappropriate training practices, and uncared-for injuries. Practice your sport with intelligent creativity and you might find yourself putting up 5.13d's like German climber Rudi Borchert did in his mid-fifties.

The Recovery Instinct

One of the most valuable things for any athlete to cultivate is an instinctive self-awareness of the recovery state of his or her body.

To develop this instinct, world-class athletes use scientific feedback methods in training or competitions to learn what it feels like when their bodies are recovered or still tired. Although this kind of monitoring is out of reach for most climbers, other methods of feedback are available.

The best measure is to keep a training log in which you note your training activities, evaluate your performance, and record your feelings. If you think it, ink it. A training journal provides a record that can help you spot patterns and learn about your recovery from different types of training.

By being aware of your training volume, recovery time, and performance throughout your day-to-day training, you'll eventually develop an instinctive feeling for how fatigued or recovered your body is. This instinct can serve as a valuable guide for when to train harder and when to back off. If it can withstand the sometimes unhealthy influence of overambitious determination and peer pressure, this instinctive sense is worth more than any other single factor in physical training.

WARMING UP

Warming up is essential to climbing your best because it prepares the three fundamental processes (psychological, motor, and autonomic) for physical activity. Blow off your warm-up or do it too fast and you burden tissues before they have the capacity to handle it. A gradual warm-up pays off by giving climbers improved endurance and energy for the rest of the day and reducing recovery time after climbing.

Warming up improves circulation by opening the capillaries that feed the muscles. Activity and blood flow warm the muscles and connective tissue, making them more elastic and injury-resistant. It also prepares the muscles' chemical environment for energy production. Warming up lubricates the joints, getting them ready for the stresses they encounter at higher intensities of exercise.

Think about how bad you are at graceful movement just after waking from a deep sleep. Just as you need a transition period to readapt yourself to moving after sleep, you need a warm-up to reacquaint your inactive nervous system with the coordination and techniques climbing demands. Since your technique won't be at its best until you're warmed up, staying off hard routes when "cold" keeps you from ingraining technique that's beneath your standards.

Changes in psychological intensity (or "arousal" in sports lingo) accompany the transition from inactivity to activity. You rarely arrive at the cliffs or the gym with the ideal level of mental intensity. If you're there for a routine workout, you're likely to be underaroused; if it's for a difficult on-sight, you're probably overaroused. A warm-up helps you to moderate psychological arousal and bring it to optimal levels.

How to Warm Up

The best warm-up for any kind of climbing is an easy version of what you'll be doing more intensely later on. A typical hike to the crag followed by two to four easier routes generally does the job.

When easy climbs aren't available, you can use a warm-up routine as a ritual that prepares you mentally and physically for climbing. Many climbers combine quick routines, like moving their joints through their ranges of motion, with easy climbs for a thorough warm-up.

A climber's warm-up routine should include the following aspects:

1. Do a general warm-up: maintain low-intensity full body activity for five minutes.

2. Move your joints through their full ranges of motion. Begin with your fingers, moving each joint individually. Continue with the wrists, elbows, and shoulders, then move through the neck, spine, hips, knees, ankles, and toes. With the shoulders and hips, be sure to not only explore the full range of motion but also roll the upper arm or thigh along its axis like an axle turning in its socket.

3. Use the muscles you'll be using later on, at a low intensity. When easy climbs are not available for this step, stretchy rubber surgical tubing comes in handy. By anchoring it below your feet, to a post, or in your other hand, you can do quick sets of several exercises against a light resistance.

4. *Lightly* stretch any tight or problem-area muscles.

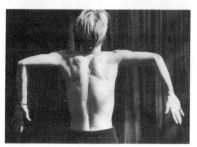

THE TEN COMMANDMENTS OF PHYSICAL TRAINING

To summarize and add to the information above, we offer our ten commandments of physical training.

1. Warm up and cool down.

For the amount of time they require, these two steps will do more to keep you healthy and improve your performance than any others.

2. Vary your climbing and training.

Variety is more than just the spice of life—it is an essential part of improving as a climber. Variety in your training means fewer injuries, better health, and better performance.

For beginning and intermediate climbers, just remember to keep your climbing diverse. Having different types of climbing days or workouts allows you to climb and train more safely: by varying the types of stress you subject yourself to, you lengthen your recovery period between any two repetitions of the same workout. Remember to have hard days *and* easy days, long days *and* short days, serious days *and* light-hearted days.

For more advanced climbers, periodization is a systematic approach to variety that helps maximize the benefits of diversity through training phases (see chapter 15).

3. Personalize your training.

Nothing works for everybody. Remember that you have a unique set of strengths and weaknesses, likes and dislikes. To be effective your training must account for your personal characteristics as well as your age and stage of athletic development.

4. Train specifically.

Make your training as specific to your climbing goals as possible. Remember that the form of training that most closely simulates the climbs you're training for will give you the best results. Specificity can involve body positions and orientations, mode (static versus dynamic), muscle contraction speed, muscle load, time of day, and other factors.

5. Increase your volume appropriately.

To improve, volume must be increased by 20 to 40 percent per year. Most climbers make this increase by raising intensity, as the difficulty of the routes they do rises over time. But if your intensity plateaus, you can always increase quantity, density, or frequency to keep yourself moving forward.

Training doesn't have to monopolize your life. Increasing just intensity and density makes ongoing improvement possible without even increasing your time commitment to climbing. But you do have to continue expecting to surpass yourself. If you *think* you've reached your limits, you almost certainly have, because you'll stop training as if you expected to get better.

6. Don't expect shortcuts.

Although conscientious training will provide you with impressive results, know that there are no miracle training plans, no shortcuts that circumvent particular stages of development. Ask any experienced and successful athlete and he'll tell you the same thing: you have to pay your dues to reap the rewards. The general rules of training apply to everyone.

7. Take time off.

Make sure you have some periods during the year when the only type of physical training you do (if any at all) is recovery training (see chapter 12, General Endurance Training). These periods should be at least a week in length and should add up to a minimum of six weeks over the course of a year.

If you refuse to include such time-off periods in your schedule or year, they'll likely force themselves upon you in the form of performance plateaus, regression, injury, or low motivation.

8. Develop a recovery instinct.

Cultivate an awareness of your state of recovery. Respect your body enough to trust that it knows what it needs. It will send you more reliable signals than any you may get from this book, from a personal trainer, or even from your own analytical mind. Because your body knows best, avoid passing judgment on its performance or response to training. You're best off being your own observer, not your own judge.

9. Stay motivated.

Don't underestimate the power of motivation. Performance and even physical strength are highly influenced by the psyche. It's hard to make ongoing gains at any type of training you hate.

You don't have to quit when you no longer enjoy every minute of training. But you should pay attention to your motivation and do what it takes to keep it on your side. Training with friends is a big motivational plus. Staying in contact with the aspects of the sport that inspire and thrill you—like visiting a certain climbing area, traveling, or just being outdoors—is equally important. Keep your flame alive.

10. Stay healthy.

There's a price to pay to avoid injuries: a boulder problem left undone, a painful finger lock you refuse to do, a crimp you decline to pull on. But the price of muscle or tendon injuries can be weeks or months of climbing. You're better off being conservative enough to avoid injuries in the first place than learning the hard way.

If you don't stay healthy, all the other principles of improving can do little to help you.

9. STRENGTH

"The only substitute for power is more power," a weary Hueco Tanks visitor once exclaimed. Although this book emphasizes that climbers too often blame shortcomings in other areas on strength deficiencies, the evidence conveyed by pumped forearms, melting fingers, and burning biceps can't be ignored. Climbing demands strength. This chapter explains the principles of strength that we'll apply to strength training in the following chapter.

Before getting to the heart of the matter, let's review some basics. The skeleton provides the framework that supports and protects the internal organs, and it is the structure on which muscles act. Muscles connect to bones via stringy attachments called tendons.

To move part of your body—to extend your arm against resistance, for example—you contract certain muscles, in this case the triceps. Your brain signals the nerve ending within the muscle. On command, the muscle fibers contract and send feedback to the brain to keep it posted on their position.

An individual muscle fiber is like a light switch: it's either on (contracted) or off (relaxed). Variations in muscle force come from having different numbers of fibers contracted. When a muscle exerts a light force, only a few fibers contract. Under heavier loads, a muscle recruits more of its fibers.

Since skeletal muscles can only make a contracting force, muscles are arranged to pull across opposite sides of a joint, so that both a flexing movement and the opposite extension can occur. The extension of the arm can happen only if the biceps (the triceps' antagonist) is relaxed. The command to extend an arm therefore signals the triceps to contract and the biceps to relax.

For a joint that moves in three dimensions, like the shoulder, a myriad of muscles surround it and work together to stabilize and direct even simple movements. This cooperative interaction between a muscle, its partners, and its antagonists to bring about movement is called intermuscular coordination. We'll discuss it further later in this chapter.

THE VARIOUS ASPECTS OF STRENGTH

Strength is the ability to exert force. When we think of how strong a muscle is, we're talking about how much force it can produce. Stronger fingers can exert a greater force to suspend weight from a hold. Stronger arms generate more force to lift or pull more weight.

In real-world climbing, however, the issue is not simply how much force you produce (your *maximum strength),* but rather how you can use your strength. Can you spend a lot of it in the concentrated period that a brief crux demands? Can you make several such moves in succession? Can you make it last the length of a pitch? The terms *power, power-endurance,* and *local endurance* describe these roles of strength in climbing. To understand and effectively develop climbing-related strengths, you must grasp these three aspects.

To illustrate them, let's look to the arena where we use them. The following chart

Grade	Route	Location	Length	The "Business"	Strength Aspect
14a	Throwin' the Houlihan	Wild Iris, Wyoming	40 feet	The first 5 moves, 5.13d	Power
14a	Dead Souls	American Fork, Utah	45 feet	15 continuous 5.12+ moves	Power-endurance
14a	To Bolt or Not to Be	Smith Rocks, Oregon	150 feet	150 feet of 5.12– cruxes	Local endurance
12d	Psycho Roof	Eldorado Canyon, Colorado	13 feet	3 move, 12d section	Power
12d	New Horizons	Button Reservoir, Colorado	45 feet	10 move, 12c section	Power-endurance
12d	Lactic Acid Bath	New River Gorge, West Virginia	75 feet	Sustained 5.11 climbing	Local endurance
12a	N.E.D.	Eldorado Canyon, Colorado	25 feet	4 move, 12a section	Power
12a	Leave It to Beaver	Joshua Tree, California	60 feet	8 move, 11c section	Power-endurance
12a	Coyne Crack	Indian Creek, Utah	70 feet	70 feet of nonstop 5.10 moves	Local endurance

Different aspects of strength in climbing routes.

shows that overall difficulty is independent of the difficulty of the crux moves, because routes of the same grade are physically demanding in completely different ways.

There are different ways a route can be physically at your limit. Power describes the rate at which we expend strength. Powerful routes require spending a lot of strength in a brief period or generating speed to make dynamic moves. Such climbing demands a maximum muscular effort for just a few moves.

By contrast, running on a flat surface for a long distance or scrambling up a mountain is an unpowerful activity, since no single movements require a rapid spending of strength. If a route's hard section is eight to twenty strenuous moves long but still at your physical limit, then the single moves must be easier than those in the last example. This type of route demands power-endurance, the muscular ability to sustain reasonably powerful efforts.

If no individual move is hard but the combination of all of them into one route gives you a pump, it tests the local endurance of the muscles involved. Local endurance refers to specific muscles' ability

Percent of maximum strength			
	25% 50%	80%	100%
Strength aspect	Local endurance	Power-endurance	Power
What it involves	Long-term use of moderate strength	Repeated use of high strength	Brief use of maximum strength
A climbing example	A long, sustained pitch with easy single moves for its grade	A short route or a sustained many-move crux	A hard boulder problem or a route with a short crux

What each aspect of strength involves.

Power-endurance involves repeated moves that feel powerful to you.

Powerful routes require brief bursts of maximum strength.

to do prolonged work at low to moderate levels of strength. (General endurance, which relates to the body's cardiovascular abilities, is covered in chapters 11 and 12.)

The chart at the bottom of page 95 shows how the aspects of strength relate to maximum strength.

We divide strength into these three aspects because each depends on particular qualities within the muscles. The figure on page 97 summarizes relationships between

On endurance routes, no single move would be hard if you were fresh; linking them to climb the route is the challenge.

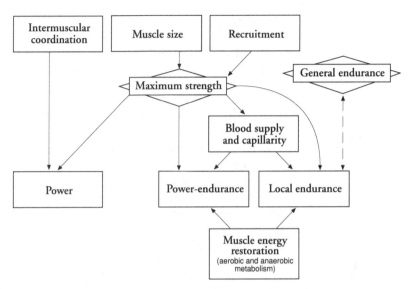

Factors influencing power, power-endurance, and local endurance.

the issues we'll discuss and serves as a graphical index to what follows.

Maximum Strength

Looking at the figure above, you'll notice the central position of maximum strength. Because it has direct effects on power, power-endurance, and local endurance, it's important to know the chief factors determining maximum strength.

Muscle Size

A muscle consists of individual muscle fibers and fat between the fibers. All other characteristics being equal, larger muscles are stronger than smaller ones.

Nevertheless, the relationship between muscle size and climbing ability is inconsistent because several other factors also affect strength. Well-trained muscles hold more stored energy (energetic phosphates and glycogen) and enzymes to use this energy than do untrained muscles. Two different muscles of the same size also can have radically different abilities to recruit the fibers they contain.

As a muscle gets bigger, its weight grows faster than its strength. If you double a muscle's weight, its strength goes up only about 60 percent. Larger muscles thus have poorer strength-to-weight ratios than smaller muscles, and people with the biggest muscles are often not as strong on rock as those with smaller frames and smaller muscles.

All uses of strength in climbing are relative to body weight. Strength in absolute terms is therefore not as important as strength relative to weight. In general, smaller and lighter people have higher relative strength which often compensates for their reach disadvantages.

Maximum Recruitment

Since contraction of an individual muscle fiber is "all or nothing," a muscle adjusts its force of contraction by changing the *number* of fibers it contracts, or "recruits." Recruitment describes the percentage of muscle fibers involved in a contraction.

The problem is that muscles have a hard time recruiting all their fibers at once. The maximum recruitment that muscles are capable of varies from person to person. Someone with poor maximum recruitment may be capable of contracting only 60 percent of the muscle fibers in a particular muscle at once. Someone with higher maximum recruitment, on the other hand, can recruit nearly all of his available muscle fibers if he exerts his maximum strength.

This explains how two people with similarly sized muscles can have radically different maximum strength, and how many top climbers can be strong despite having relatively small muscles. With poor recruitment, there's a deficit between your maximum strength and your potential strength.

Because recruitment determines the power your muscles can produce, it is an extremely important issue in climbing. The ideal climber would have only moderately sized muscles (to limit body weight) but a high level of recruitment. Fortunately, recruitment is a trainable factor.

High recruitment can be a dangerous advantage, however. On one hand, the ability to recruit more fibers can get you through more powerful single moves. On the other, it gives you the potential to consume (and thus deplete) muscle energy much faster than a person with poor recruitment.

It takes experience and practice to use only the strength that a route calls for and nothing more. To a climber lacking the technique or psychological poise to use the minimum amount of energy to get past a

Muscle fibers playing tug of war.

crux, high maximum recruitment can be more a curse than a blessing.

We'll discuss training techniques for improving recruitment in chapter 10, Strength Training. Now let's look at how maximum strength combines with other factors to influence the climbing-specific strengths, power, power-endurance, and local endurance.

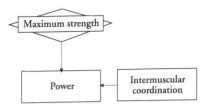

How Intermuscular Coordination Affects Power

In climbing, power output never relies on just one or two muscles. Instead, powerful moves require the coordinated synchronization and timing of many muscles working together.

As a climber's body pulls past a hold, different muscles must be used to maintain a constant force on it. If his muscles lack a *balance* of strength, he won't be able to move fluidly through these transitions. Since balanced contributions of muscle force make movement possible, the weakest muscle in the group being used often limits power on rock.

Intermuscular coordination is the term used to describe this balance. It stands apart from the other muscular qualities we'll examine in this chapter because no single muscle has it.

Max once went on a weight training craze for eight months in an effort to increase his strength. The muscles he targeted gained significant strength, and his biceps, triceps, and lats had never felt or looked better. When he got back into climbing, however, he developed twinges of pain and muscle pulls in his wrists and shoulders. What went wrong?

Our joints are surrounded by numerous small muscles that adjust and steer the forces exerted by the larger "workhorse" muscles. They lack the strength and size of the more glamorous muscles, but they play a crucial role in the control of all movements. To do their job, the strength of these stabilizing muscles must stay in proportion to the larger muscles they work with. Although his weight training had isolated and significantly increased the strength of Max's larger muscles, its limited ranges of movement failed to develop his stabilizing muscles for the more active role they play in climbing. When he returned to rock, where the diversity of positions and moves called upon his weak stabilizers to manage his formidable muscles, they weren't up to the job.

The value of climbing-specific intermuscular coordination explains why the hardest routes have involved the most specific training. *Hubble, Action Direct,* and *Just Do It,* the only three 8c+'s at this writing, were climbed only after precise simulation training for the specific movements they require.

How Maximum Strength Affects Power

You have to be able to generate a lot of force to hang or pull on certain holds. If you lack maximum strength, you won't be able to do powerful moves and sequences. But deficiencies in maximum strength affect power in more subtle ways too.

One way maximum strength affects climbing power is through *contact strength.* Contact strength is the ability to exert high force on contact with a hold; it is measured by how long it takes after initiating a contraction to develop one's maximum strength. Dynamic moves to poor holds often require good contact strength: if your fingers can't muster their strength quickly, you're likely to fall off.

When we try to turn on our strength, the development of force is not instantaneous. Climbers with poor contact strength may require a second or more of gradual force increase before achieving their maximum strength. High contact strength climbers, on the other hand, can produce their maximum strength in a fraction of that time. The delay is a function of a muscle's maximum recruitment. Contact strength and maximum strength are the two best reasons for climbers to develop high recruitment in their muscles.

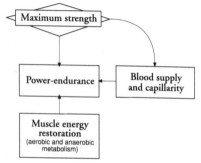

François Dreyfus demonstrating contact strength on his ascent of Agincourt.

Power-endurance
Restoring Muscle Energy

Adenosine triphosphate (ATP) and other phosphates are the energy compounds muscles rely on to contract. Because they're difficult to store, muscles contain only enough for about five seconds of full contraction. Sustained muscle contractions thus rely on the metabolic (energy-restoring) processes that replenish ATP.

As the muscle consumes ATP, it manufactures more from stored glycogen. Muscles can do this *aerobically* or *anaerobically* — with or without oxygen. Aerobic metabolism burns stored muscle sugar (glycogen) efficiently, producing the most ATP possible from it. Since it needs oxygen to do so, however, it requires a steady supply of blood— something not always available while climbing.

When you climb powerful moves, the oxygen-carrying blood supply is blocked (we'll see why in a moment), and muscles often need more ATP than they can produce solely by aerobic metabolism. In these circumstances cells resort to making ATP anaerobically. Anaerobic metabolism is a less effective but better-than-nothing form of ATP restoration that works without oxygen.

Anaerobic metabolism burns glycogen incompletely, leaving lactic acid as an end product of the reaction. Chemical principles tell us that as end products accumulate in any chemical reaction, the rate of that reaction decreases. In other words, if you don't

remove the ash, it'll smother the fire. Similarly, the accumulation of lactic acid slows ATP restoration.

Because aerobic metabolism makes complete use of glycogen, generating more ATP with less waste, the body prefers it to the anaerobic path. So why would muscles want to use the lactic-acid-producing anaerobic pathway? They're forced to resort to it because blood supply is limited at some of the times the muscles most need ATP.

The Blood Blockade

When a muscle contracts, the tightening of its fibers squeezes the capillaries that supply it. As contraction increases, it eventually pinches shut its own capillaries. So the amount of blood available to the muscle fibers depends on just how contracted the muscle is.

In easy climbing, where the load on a muscle is less than 20 percent of its maxi-

Load (percent of maximum strength)		
0%　　　20%　　　　50%　　　　　　100%		

Blood vessels	Fully open	Partially open	Completely shut
Metabolic pathway	Aerobic only	Aerobic and anaerobic	Anaerobic only
Maximum holding time	Indefinite	Decreasing	40 to 90 seconds

The effect of muscle load on blood delivery and metabolic pathway.

mum strength, capillaries open fully, allowing unrestricted blood flow. Fresh blood loaded with oxygen and sugar easily reaches the muscle cells. The aerobic pathway prevails, full use of glycogen occurs, and no lactic acid accumulates. In these conditions, you *can't* get pumped.

When a climb is more difficult and the load on muscles rises to between 20 and 50 percent, the contraction of a muscle's fibers partially closes its capillaries. This slows blood flow, limits oxygen delivery, and thus hinders aerobic metabolism. To meet the muscle's energy needs, some ATP must be produced anaerobically, with lactic acid as a byproduct. This type of climbing produces the feeling of muscle fatigue climbers call a pump.

On powerful sections of climbing that require 50 percent or more of a muscle's maximum contraction, tightening of the muscle completely shuts the capillaries feeding it. The figure on page 101 illustrates the changes in capillary size at different loads.

With all blood flow blockaded, the muscle can only restore ATP anaerobically. Lactic acid accumulates, and the muscle fatigues quickly, since blood can neither replace the consumed energy nor remove the accumulating lactic acid. Until the muscle relaxes or its load drops below 50 percent of its maximum strength, no blood goes in or out of the muscle. If uninterrupted, the lactic acid build-up halts muscle energy restoration within forty to ninety seconds, and the muscle fails. For a climber hanging on a hold at this intensity, his forearms fill with lactic acid until his fingers open up against his will.

Fortunately, we don't hang on the same holds continuously. Forearm muscles operate in a "static-intermittent" mode, alternating between static contractions while holding on and relaxation while reaching between holds. On powerful routes, where capillaries close shut with every hold, the only chance to remove lactic acid and enable continued energy restoration is while the hand reaches for the next hold. Therefore it's crucial that full benefit of these instants is not sabotaged by any psychological or physical tension that prevents the muscles from relaxing between holds. (See the section on Progressive Muscle Relaxation in chapter 7.)

How Maximum Strength Affects Power-endurance

The role of blood flow in energy restoration explains the impact of maximum strength on one's endurance. The accompanying figure shows why. On a two-centimeter edge, Max can produce a maximum of ninety-six pounds of force in his fingers, whereas Julia can exert only fifty pounds. Imagine a route where every hold is this size and requires twenty-three pounds of finger force from a person of Julia and Max's weight. This represents 46 percent of Julia's maximum strength. Her capillaries will be almost completely shut by this effort, and her forearms will quickly accumulate an incapacitating amount of lactic acid.

For Max, however, this level of force represents only 23 percent of his maximum strength. Although he may produce a small portion of his muscle energy anaerobically (with lactic acid as waste), his capillaries will be almost fully open, so removing it won't

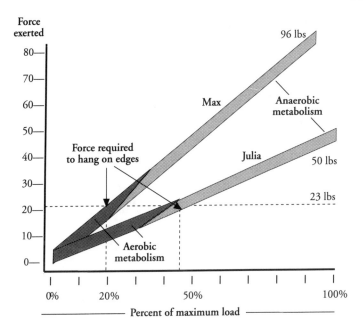

The effect of maximum strength on power-endurance.

pose a problem. He could climb at this intensity almost indefinitely. A reasonable local endurance route for Max (he stays unpumped, restoring energy aerobically at a low percentage of his maximum strength) is a strenuous power-endurance route for Julia (since it demands fairly powerful moves for her, she must restore energy anaerobically, and she gets pumped).

Note that this route demands much less than either climber's maximum strength. But because maximum strength affects capillary closure, it impacts both power-endurance and local endurance. This also hints at the importance of a well-developed network of capillaries to deliver and remove blood to and from the muscles.

Understanding a Forearm Pump

Knowing how energy is restored in working muscles explains why a forearm pump accompanies power-endurance work. During muscle activity, ATP is used not to contract fibers but rather to reset a contracted fiber to a relaxed state. Once relaxed, the fiber is "cocked" and needs no ATP to fire. It's ready to go. Muscles are like mousetraps: *preparing* each fiber to contract requires ATP, but *releasing* that energy only takes a neural signal. This is why dead bodies exhibit rigor mortis. With ATP restoration halted the muscles can't relax, and they remain permanently contracted.

In power-endurance activities, ATP shortages cause fibers to stay contracted

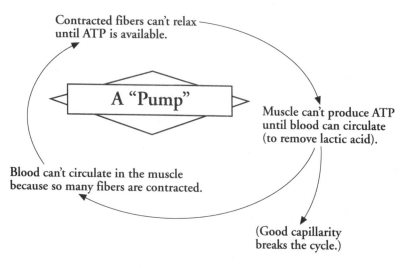

Contracted fibers can't relax until ATP is available.

A "Pump"

Muscle can't produce ATP until blood can circulate (to remove lactic acid).

Blood can't circulate in the muscle because so many fibers are contracted.

(Good capillarity breaks the cycle.)

The cycle that causes a pump.

after firing. This causes a muscle hardening not unlike rigor mortis. Here's how it happens: high load use closes off capillaries, but the determined climber pushes onward. If muscles keep consuming ATP until lactic acid stalls energy restoration, they're trapped in a vicious circle. The many contracted fibers can't relax without ATP around. ATP can't be produced until blood circulates (to remove the lactic acid). Blood can't flow

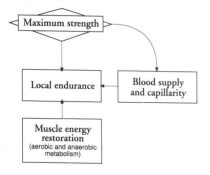

Maximum strength

Local endurance

Blood supply and capillarity

Muscle energy restoration
(aerobic and anaerobic metabolism)

into the muscle because so many fibers are contracted.

This cycle explains why beginners find it so hard to shake off a real pump. Their underdeveloped capillary network inhibits blood's infiltration into tightened muscles. The well-trained climber's superior capillarity breaks this cycle more quickly. We'll have more to say about capillarity in a moment.

Local Endurance

Don't confuse local endurance with the cardiovascular abilities that give rise to general endurance. We'll consider general endurance later in the book.

Local endurance refers to the ability of the specific muscles involved in climbing to maintain a moderate level of work for an extended period. Since local endurance involves sustained muscle use, it too is essentially an energy problem. You can endure

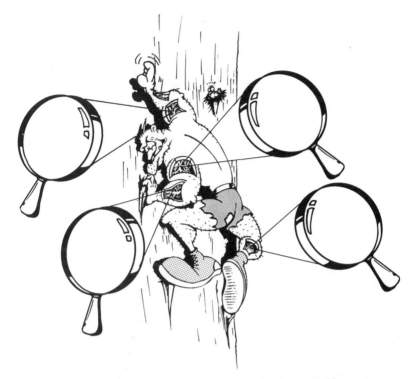

Bruno's free arm is temporarily relaxed as it reaches for the next hold. Its veins are fully open, and bring the muscle oxygen and carry away lactic acid accumulated during the previous hold. Since it hasn't had a constant supply of oxygen, much of the arm's energy restoration is anaerobic. Bruno's lock-off muscles are operating at 40 percent of maximum strength. Capillaries in these muscles are constricted, but not closed altogether. With the restricted blood supply, not all the energy can be restored aerobically. Some is restored anaerobically, and a moderate pump is developing as a result. Gripping a small edge, Bruno's forearms are contracted at 80 percent of their maximum strength. The capillaries within these muscles are completely shut, so muscle energy is restored anaerobically, lactic acid is accumulating, and Bruno's forearms feel "pumped." Bruno's calves are working at 20 percent of their maximum strength. All their energy needs can be met aerobically. As a result they don't fatigue or feel pumped.

as long as your muscles can reproduce the energy they consume for contraction.

Because endurance climbing involves easy individual moves, muscle loads are lower than in power-endurance climbing. This lower intensity creates different working conditions within the muscles, and some of the problems associated with power-endurance climbing don't occur. Specifically, the muscles have much better access to blood at the loads that characterize endurance climbing. As a result, a much higher proportion of the muscle's ATP can be produced aerobically.

Local endurance abilities thus depend on three factors: the effect of maximum strength on capillary closure (discussed above), capillarity, and the efficiency of the aerobic energy restoration pathway. We've already discussed item one above. Let's have a closer look at items two and three.

Capillarity

Capillaries are the vital "supply lines" that support muscle exertion. When they provide the blood a working muscle needs, you can keep using your muscles without a pump, and they feel fresh. But when more blood is needed than they're capable of carrying, or they get pinched shut by strong contractions, the muscles starve for oxygen and fatigue.

When muscles are inactive, these flexible blood-carrying passageways are narrow, and many of them are closed altogether. When a muscle is active, capillaries stretch, widening to handle the extra blood they carry to support energy restoration.

When capillaries frequently accommodate the extra quantities and pressures of blood that accompany local endurance work, they widen and multiply to adapt to the needs of exercise. The result can be literally miles of new blood-supply networks infiltrating your muscles. The new, denser capillary networks deliver oxygen and remove lactic acid much more quickly than those in untrained muscles, enabling muscles to restore consumed energy faster. As a result you can climb harder routes without getting pumped, and you can recover faster when you do get pumped.

Unfortunately, not all the physical changes made in capillarity are permanent. When muscles go unused, capillarity diminishes.

Aerobic Metabolism

Effective training improves the efficiency of aerobic ATP restoration. Demanding a maximum of aerobic energy restoration in training causes muscle cells to build new components, store more energy reserves, and change their chemistry to enable a more rapid conversion of glycogen to ATP.

In the Strength Training chapter we'll consider ways of training the aerobic systems within muscles and improving capillarity.

Trade-offs

It's important to remember that any kind of training you do will affect more than just the abilities it involves most directly. Your body responds holistically to training.

The spinoff of this principle here is that endurance training reduces the maximum recruitment of muscles. So it can lower your maximum strength and power because you lose the ability to recruit as many fibers.

If you think about it from your body's viewpoint, this change makes sense. Through endurance training, your body is "told" to adapt to climbing for longer periods. Reducing recruitment is a good way to ensure that it will be able to do so. Lowering recruitment to limit a muscle's maximum strength is like putting a doorstop under your car's gas pedal. It keeps you from being able to rocket out of a stoplight, but it ensures that you'll get farther on a tank of gas.

In the best of both worlds you'd have free rein on the gas pedal *and* the discipline to conserve your energy when you can. We want *both* maximum strength and high endurance. This will only benefit you if you have the technical skill and discipline to avoid wasting your extra strength through inefficient climbing. And maximizing both maximum strength and endurance is possible only if your training is properly periodized (see chapter 15).

OTHER FACTORS INFLUENCING STRENGTH

Psychological State

As discussed in the psychology chapters, strength is sensitive to arousal level. You won't be as strong in more relaxed states as when you're highly aroused. But higher arousal levels trade coordination for strength gains.

Autonomic Reserves

The final 5 to 10 percent of our maximum strength is protected from easy access. These "autonomic reserves" are accessible only in times of crisis or situations of extraordinary psychological intensity. Mothers dip into these reserves to lift cars off their children in emergencies.

We are prohibited from using our autonomic reserves on a day-to-day basis, because tapping them pushes us up to and sometimes beyond our physical limits and has repercussions on the body. Top climbers have been reduced to states of lethargy following performances where they used their bodies close to their true physical limits.

Planning to access these reserves requires that the desired event develop enormous psychological proportions to the athlete. And even this doesn't guarantee peak performance unless the other abilities that bear on climbing are also maximized.

Injury and Micro-trauma

Muscular sites of injury or excessive micro-trauma are vulnerable because they're spots of weakness. They're likely sites of further damage if subjected to maximum contractions. As a result, damaged muscles apparently limit their maximum strength by reducing their recruitment. This is one reason why overtraining and injuries reduce strength.

10. STRENGTH TRAINING

Each of us has different propensities for the different aspects of strength. Max, for example, has naturally high recruitment and impresses his partners with his short bursts of climbing power. Julia has a more endurance-oriented body, weaker on hard single moves but strong on long pitches.

These differences highlight the advantage of learning about the principles of strength training and how they apply on the rock, as opposed to memorizing a specific workout or two. Equipped with understanding, a climber can create effective training programs emphasizing his particular needs. In what follows, we'll look at how you acquire the various aspects of strength we discussed in the last chapter.

To understand the language of strength training, there are a few terms you should know. Although they came from gym weight training, we'll apply them to the rock as well.

Unlike the steady-state activity that characterizes general endurance workouts, strength training typically involves alternating between bursts of activity aimed at fatiguing specific muscles and periods of rest. A *set* is one such interval of activity. The ideal length of the rests separating sets depends on the type of training.

A set typically consists of one or more movements that are repeated for the duration of the set. Each of these motions is called a *repetition* (or rep). A climber doing three sets of pullups with seven repetitions each would do a total of twenty-one pullups.

Recovery time refers to how long it takes for the targeted muscles to recover from the stress of a workout and be prepared for another. The ideal recovery time varies depending on the nature and intensity of the workout.

The *load* refers to the weight a muscle must contract against. It is often expressed as a percentage of maximum strength. For example, Julia can do a pullup with a maximum of 30 extra pounds attached to her waist. Her maximum strength, therefore, is 30 pounds plus her body weight, or 160 pounds. When she does pullups without extra weight, the load is roughly 130 pounds, which is 81 percent of her maximum strength.

Phase length, as we'll use it in this book, refers to the ideal duration, usually in weeks, to concentrate on a particular training phase. Any shorter than the duration we specify and you won't have long enough to improve; any longer and you'll plateau in your rate of improvement.

INTERMUSCULAR COORDINATION

Since intermuscular coordination reflects the muscles' balance of development and ability to work together, any type of training we'll discuss will either promote or reduce it.

To develop muscle strength in the proportions that climbing demands, one's training must simulate as closely as possible the movements made in climbing. The body's physical adaptations are specific to the speeds, positions, and angles of force involved in training. Climbing, therefore, is the best intermuscular training for climbers.

Does this mean that climbing is the only way to develop worthwhile strength? Not necessarily. As we'll see in a moment, other forms of training can more rapidly improve specific aspects of muscular strength. Just remember that climbing will best weave the strength gains made through other types of training back together, balancing them into proportions that will serve your ability on rock. When feasible, training methods that use climbing exercises to target the aspects of strength you need will usually give you the best results.

MAXIMUM STRENGTH

In the strength chapter, we discussed the central importance of maximum strength and its influence on the climbing-related strength aspects, power, power-endurance, and local endurance. Since maximum strength depends on muscle size and maximum recruitment, these are the focuses of the two methods aimed at increasing it.

Increasing Muscle Size: Hypertrophy Training

Hypertrophy training prompts muscles to increase their size partly by draining their reserves of energetic compounds that restore ATP (the chemical muscles rely on to contract). It accomplishes this by exercising muscles to the point of failure with intermediate loads and rests short enough to prevent significant restoration of these reserves.

Hypertrophy Training through Climbing

Climbing causes muscle hypertrophy, especially when muscles are worked to the point of failure. But climbing doesn't produce the fastest size gains. Since each move on a route uses different positions and muscle combinations, individual muscles are not pushed consistently to the point of failure.

Since successive moves are rarely identical, fatigue shifts from one muscle group to the next, allowing partial recovery of some groups nearing failure. So simultaneous failure of all the muscles involved is unlikely, and the climber usually falls off when only one or a few muscles fail. Since climbing requires significant coordination, climbers also fall off when muscular fatigue drops their coordination too far. As a result, climbers often stop a climbing "set" before fatigue of any one muscle group reaches the level of fatigue optimal for hypertrophy.

To maximize the hypertrophy effects in climbing training, look for routes that are repetitive in the types of moves and holds they involve. Look for sequences that will make you reach muscular failure within ten to twenty-five seconds. (When subsequent moves are varied, this time duration must increase for hypertrophic gains.) If you can find several routes near each other, using a slightly easier route for each subsequent "set" can help you maintain a constant set duration as you fatigue.

Hypertrophy Training on Fingerboards

For a hypertrophy workout on a fingerboard, follow the guidelines in the hypertrophy overview table to plan your sets and your load. Through trial and error, adjust the amount of weight you hang from the holds by suspending weights from a harness you wear or by standing in elastic bands. Aim

Hypertrophy Training Overview			
	Beginner	Intermediate	Advanced
Load	40–60%	60–80%	80–85%
Repetitions	8–12	6–10	5–6
Duration	15 seconds	10 seconds	6 seconds
Sets	4–6	6–8	6–10
Rest between sets	4 minutes	3–4 minutes	2–3 minutes
Should feel	Painful during last two repetitions		
Recovery time	48–60 hours		
Phase length	4–8 weeks		

Adjust your load so that you fail at the desired number of repetitions.

to find the weight that will make your sets last the duration prescribed.

Alternatively, you can accurately determine your load by first figuring out your maximum strength on the holds you plan to use. Do this by finding out the most weight you can suspend from the hold for at least two seconds (body weight plus any extra you add with weights, or minus whatever you take off with elastics). Determine what your chosen percentage of the maximum load is, and then make yourself that weight by adding or subtracting weight with extra weights or elastics.

To fully deplete energy stores, use the same hold for the duration of a set. For example, you might shift weight back and forth between your right and left hands for the duration of each set without changing the hold that each hand grips. Or you can hang statically from the same one or two holds for the duration of the set.

Because hypertrophy training on fingerboards targets a specific muscle group (the fingers and forearms), it warrants some particular considerations. Because of the forearms' small size and the fact that they're a focus of muscular demands in nearly all types of climbing, forearm muscles are frequently overtrained by climbers.

When muscle bulk grows faster than other structures can adapt to, problems like carpal tunnel syndrome can result. More common is a milder level of overtraining in which the forearm muscles simply never have time to catch up and recover from the stresses they experience. This not only stalls improvement but also can produce muscle scar tissue that permanently hampers further gains. Hypertrophy on the fingerboard is therefore only appropriate during periods when you're not doing much difficult climbing.

Because of their finger emphasis, fingerboards offer little to the upper arm or back muscles. If you're doing pullups on the fingerboard, for example, you're unlikely to fatigue both the upper arm and forearm muscles to failure simultaneously.

Hypertrophy Training off the Wall

Weight training produces the quickest hypertrophy gains because it can isolate one or a few muscles at a time and work them to failure. Since weight training requires little coordination, it pushes muscles much closer to absolute fatigue than climbing can.

The minimal coordination required in weight training is both its advantage and its disadvantage. It allows for quicker size gains, but it fails to develop technique and intermuscular coordination as muscles grow. If hypertrophic weight training is used only as a phase in a wider program of more climbing-specific training, it can be a valuable addition to many climbers'

training. We'll have more to say about incorporating it with other phases in the Scheduling and Periodization chapter.

If you need ideas for weight training exercise, several body-building books describe exercises targeting the different muscles. By using such exercises according to the schemes we describe here, you will achieve your strength goals.

Machines or Free Weights?

Because strength gains are so specific to the movements involved in training, it's important to choose training mediums and exercises that best duplicate climbing's positions and moves. For this reason, free weights are usually preferable to machines.

Because they're fixed in one plane of activity, machines eliminate the need to stabilize and adjust the path taken in an exercise. As a result, they fail to develop the stabilizing and supporting muscles that adjust the course and rotations of our moving limbs.

Other Aspects of Hypertrophy Training

Since weight grows faster than strength, more muscle is not always better. Hypertrophy training only makes sense until an

optimum ratio of maximum strength to weight is reached. Smaller climbers can typically afford to add bulk without nearing this "mixed-blessing" threshold. But large-muscled bodies should target only the muscles that truly need strengthening. Burly climbers are typically better off focusing on other aspects of strength.

Hypertrophy warrants a higher priority in the earlier phases of climbers' development than it does at later stages, when emphasis is more profitably shifted to the other components of strength.

During a hypertrophy program, trust that gains are occurring even if the visual results are less than shocking: if you increase a muscle's mass by a dramatic 30 percent, its thickness may increase only 15 percent.

Remember too that hypertrophy is not the end goal. Although hypertrophy training will contribute to a muscle's maximum strength, it may not exhibit any effects on *climbing* power. Hypertrophy produces big "dumb" muscles. Until the other factors contributing to power on rock are addressed (recruitment and intermuscular coordination), any measurable gains in absolute strength may be offset by weight gains.

Maximum Recruitment Training

Recruitment training aims to increase the percentage of a muscle's fibers you can recruit at will. Where hypertrophy developed quantity, recruitment training breeds quality. Recruitment training should add appreciably to your maximum strength, though your muscles may actually get smaller in the process.

Using loads close to the limits of your maximum strength forces a muscle to use as many fibers as it can. When you repeat this demand, the body gets better at recruiting its fibers.

The eccentric phase of a movement (for example, releasing from a pullup to a hanging position) makes the greatest stimulus for increasing recruitment. Some advanced recruitment exercises we'll discuss below (forced negatives and reactive training) take advantage of this by increasing the load on a repetition's negative phase to loads heavier than the muscles are capable of lifting.

Maximum Recruitment Training through Climbing

Because climbing frequently involves powerful single moves, it increases maximum recruitment. A recent German study showed that sport climbers had the highest recruitment in upper body muscle groups of all athletes measured (Radlinger, 1987).

The biggest stumbling block to maximum recruitment training through climbing and bouldering is that finger skin often wears out before a sufficient training stimulus is reached. When skin friction on the roughness of holds is part of what maintains contact, high load efforts are likely to wear skin thin.

The increasingly popular homemade wooden bouldering structures offer one solution. Wooden holds put almost no stress on the finger skin and minimize the chances that pain will interfere with maximum intensity efforts.

■ **On Routes.** Effective maximum recruitment training requires sequences of no more than six movements and a recovered state of freshness before beginning each effort. For this reason, training recruitment on climbs typically involves only short portions of a particular route. This type of training can take place as a climber rehearses a difficult route he hopes to redpoint.

To maximize the recruitment effects, break the crux sections into lengths appropriate to your skill level according to the maximum recruitment overview table. Take an adequate rest between efforts.

■ **Bouldering.** Powerful bouldering is the best form of maximum recruitment training for climbers. Although it's not as easy to calculate exact loads as it is in weight training, the value of bouldering's specificity far outweighs this disadvantage.

Look for boulder problems with single moves that demand your maximum strength. Each move in a one- to six-move sequence should be of a maximum difficulty for you. Using techniques like taking weight off (see chapter 4) will help you learn to climb the hardest possible problems for you, and eventually help you achieve maximum muscle loads.

Powerful bouldering is the best way for climbers to train maximum recruitment.

Opt for problems where it takes pure finger strength rather than skin friction to stick to the holds. (As mentioned above, wooden bouldering structures are ideal for this.)

Maximum Recruitment Training Overview			
	Beginner	Intermediate	Advanced
Load	Inappropriate	80–90%	90–150%
Repetitions		3–6	1–3
Sets		6–8	6–10
Rest between sets		3–5 minutes	3–5 minutes
Should feel	Too brief to cause any painful muscle fatigue		
Recovery time	48–72 hours or even more		
Phase length	2–5 weeks		

Maximum Recruitment Training on Fingerboards

To train maximum recruitment on fingerboards, target only your finger strength. If you try to do high-load pullups on small edges, you're unlikely to push both your finger strength *and* your pullup strength to the point of muscle failure.

For a fingerboard workout, add or subtract an appropriate weight from your body so that you can sustain the holds for two to six seconds before your muscles fail. Each of these holding periods constitutes one set.

■ Wolfgang Güllich's "Reactive Training."

Germany's top redpoint climber used this high-intensity form of recruitment training to successfully prepare for one of the hardest routes in the world, *Action Direct*. When he first tried the route, Wolfgang couldn't even hang on its one-finger pockets, let alone muster the contact strength to latch them after the long dynos required to reach between them. Since his base level of fitness was already at the peak of strength development, adding the necessary strength required an extreme technique.

For his finger training, Wolfgang used an oversized wooden fingerboard with sloping edges and rounded rungs running horizontally across it. The holds were too sloping to be held as closed crimps and required either an open crimp or extended grip. Because of the difficulty of holding them, reaching from one to another required a precise deadpoint, with the body's plane of acceleration—positioned beneath the handhold sought—melding coordination and power training.

To use the reactive method, Wolfgang would dyno to a higher edge, with one or more fingers on each edge, then drop back down to catch himself on the lower edge. Dropping onto holds demands maximum contact strength, and muscles are temporarily lengthened under high loads as they strain to hold on. This lengthening under load improves nerve connections to otherwise inactivated muscle fibers (thanks to the muscle spindle reflex), boosting recruitment.

Because of the high intensities involved, this training method flirts dangerously with injury. *Never use reactive training more than twice a week.* But if you have climbed hard for at least six years and want to activate every fiber possible, this is the method to use. It will improve your power on hard brief-crux climbing problems.

Maximum Recruitment Training off the Wall

Weight training offers the convenience of careful measurability and easy adjustability of loads. For a maximum recruitment workout with weights, choose just two to four exercises focusing on movements that require the most power in climbing.

Since this phase should come close to the performance phase (see chapter 15), seek exercises that encourage intermuscular cooperation in climbing-specific ways rather than isolating single muscles.

For example, a weight training recruitment workout could consist of:

- A thorough warm-up of low-intensity upper body weight exercises
- Eight sets of three maximum-intensity repetitions in the following three

exercises: pullups, dips, and single-arm rows
• Light warm-down exercises.

Since speed is one component of power, some Soviet trainers suggest following maximum-load efforts by six to ten repetitions of lighter loads (30 to 50 percent of maximum strength) done as quickly as possible. Go as fast as you can, but retain enough precision to ensure that your muscles (and not your joints) support the load at the ends of the range of motion.

For the experienced weight lifter, 150-percent loads can be achieved through "forced negatives." Since 100 percent is by definition the maximum load you can contract against, loads exceeding 100 percent involve resisting higher loads through the negative, or eccentric, phase of a repetition. For example, a partner may support an extra weight strapped to a climber during the concentric phase of a pullup, releasing it when the climber is at the top of the pullup to burden him with more weight as he lowers down than he could have pulled up. This is also the foundation of reactive training.

Other Aspects of Maximum Recruitment Training

Since you're unlikely to measure your maximum recruitment in one of former East Germany's performance labs, use common sense. If you look like Tarzan, with twenty-inch biceps, but you can only do a pullup with as much additional load as the skinny kid at the climbing gym, you have poor maximum recruitment. On the other hand, if your maximum strength is unusual for someone with muscles your size, you're a

high-recruitment climber. Most people fall somewhere between these two extremes.

A maximum recruitment phase is always a smart follow-up to a hypertrophy program, because it converts new bulky muscles to efficient, usable ones that provide the maximum possible strength.

Because of the high loads involved, it pays to ease into maximum recruitment training gradually. Pyramid training, discussed below, is one way to do this. For the same reason, thorough warming up is especially important in maximum recruitment training. Take at least twenty minutes to warm up the muscles and joints your workout will involve. Even once warm, athletes often don't show their maximum strength until their second or sometimes third set of an exercise.

Be sure to allow yourself the full recovery time suggested. Recovery times are exceptionally long for recruitment training because it stresses the entire neuromuscular system.

Combining Hypertrophy and Recruitment: Pyramids

Pyramid training combines the effects of hypertrophy and recruitment training through a series of sets that become progressively more intense. This type of training is appropriate in two general situations. For a climber who lacks the time for a complete phase dedicated to each focus, it gives him some of the benefits of both hypertrophy and recruitment training. Second, for a climber switching from hypertrophy to recruitment training, a week or so of pyramids can smooth the transition and prepare the body for the intense loads recruitment training involves.

Pyramid Overview	
Load, repetitions, and sets	See table below
Rest between sets	3–4 minutes
Recovery time	48–72 hours
Phase length	1–5 weeks

The pyramid training guide table presents some different pyramids and shows how you would do a series of sets of a particular exercise. For example, if you chose to do standard pyramids for three exercises (dips, pullups, and rows), you would (after a warm-up) do a set of five dips, a set of four dips, a set of three dips, a set of two dips, and another set of two dips. For each set, you adjust the load so you fail at the desired number of repetitions. Then you would repeat the pyramid process for pullups and then for rows.

The table also serves as a guideline for how many repetitions to expect from your-self at different percentages of your maximum strength. For example, at 80 percent of your maximum strength, you can expect to do about four repetitions of any exercise before reaching failure.

MUSCULAR ENERGY RESTORATION

Muscles' abilities to produce ATP by both the aerobic and anaerobic pathways can be improved through training, by creating situations that demand a maximum of energy production and limit the roles of other aspects of strength. Training the energy production system thus involves pushing at the limits of the muscles' ability to restore muscle energy.

Training gains in energy production are *very* specific, not only to the muscles being trained but also to the positions, speeds, and modes (static versus dynamic) in which they're used. This means that gains made in your legs through running will have little effect on your forearm muscles. Even metabolic forearm gains made on crimpy

Pyramid Training Guide			
Percentage of maximum strength	Recruitment emphasis	Standard pyramid	Hypertrophy emphasis
60%			1 set of 8 reps
65%			1 set of 7 reps
70%			1 set of 6 reps
75%		1 set of 5 reps	1 set of 5 reps
80%	1 set of 4 reps	1 set of 4 reps	2 sets of 4 reps
85%	1 set of 3 reps	1 set of 3 reps	
90%	1 set of 2 reps	2 sets of 2 reps	
95–100%	2 sets of 1 rep		

routes will not transfer well to open-handed climbing.

Anaerobic climbing is most sensitive to training specificity, because in climbing that is difficult enough to shut your capillaries, there are often only one or two positions in which you can make each move. If these movements are not of a style you trained, it's tough luck for you.

The easier-move climbing that typifies situations of aerobic energy restoration gives you a greater margin to climb with your preferred finger or body positions. Specificity in local aerobic training is thus not as important as for anaerobic training, because it's more likely that you'll be able to use the styles and positions at which you honed your metabolic abilities.

Anaerobic Energy Restoration

Training that targets anaerobic abilities focuses its demands on the muscle systems that restore ATP when blood and oxygen are scarce. It therefore requires loads high enough that capillaries feeding the muscles are mostly shut, yet low enough that the exercise can persist long enough to constitute a significant training stimulus.

This is one type of training where the saying "No pain no gain" really does apply. When you're training the anaerobic systems properly, you'll feel the burning, painful pump that masochistic climbers revere. This feeling comes from the pre-rigor-mortis state that ATP-starved muscles reach when their fibers can't relax. To demand the most of the anaerobic systems, you flirt with muscular failure.

When you've finished an anaerobic training session, your muscles will feel tight, hard, and unable to do more work for some time.

Local Anaerobic Training Overview	
Load	50–80%
Duration	1½–4 minutes
Repetitions or moves	20–30
Sets	1–4
Rest between sets	3–5 minutes
Should feel	A sustained, burning, painful pump
Recovery time	48–72 hours
Phase length	2–4 weeks

Anaerobic Training through Climbing

Remember to apply the fundamental principles of technique training (see chapter 3) to maximize your anaerobic training benefits from climbing. You don't learn technique well when you're tired and uncoordinated. So for optimum development of technique, avoid this type of training on routes involving techniques you're unskilled at. Staying on routes you know enhances your power-endurance training and spares your technique from any damage. When you can, opt for strength-dependent styles of climbs.

Another fine point: while you're climbing, don't *try* to get this anaerobic pump. Climbing is about *avoiding* getting pumped. So even when you train the anaerobic system, try not to get such a pump, but train on routes that force it on you.

■ **On Routes.** Look for routes where the moves all feel powerful to you yet are feasible enough that you can do at least three minutes of them before reaching

Lock-off training builds strength in the positions from which climbers scan for holds and work with protection.

muscular failure. Sustained routes are best for anaerobic training, but even on routes that intersperse easy and hard climbing you can skip rest holds to sustain a constant level of intensity. Top-roping is a wise choice for anaerobic training on routes, since lactic acid severely reduces physical coordination.

■ **"Le Travail d'Hercule"—J. B. Tribout's Lock-off Training.** Top French climbers were the first to use this training method to build anaerobic strength in the positions from which climbers "scan" for holds or clip protection. *Le principe est simple:* as you progress up a route, pause during each reach to a subsequent hold, floating your hand over it for two to five seconds before finally grabbing it.

By focusing fatigue on specific muscles and positions, lock-off training not only adds anaerobic training emphasis to the upper arms and back but also helps teach the optimal body positions and orientations for moves. In addition, it strengthens the core muscles that stabilize your body in the difficult positions that long lock-offs require.

Be warned that such training builds the habit of static, controlled climbing. If you already have a very static climbing style, you might benefit more from the one-arm traverse exercise discussed in the next section.

■ **Bouldering.** A good way to make a bouldering routine anaerobic is by combining several difficult boulder problems that you've done on previous occasions. Find ways to down-climb moderate holds from the end of one problem to the start of the next, stringing together three to five problems at a time.

If you can find a wall with enough big holds, one-arm traverses are also excellent for this type of training for climbers of intermediate and advanced ability. The Technique Training chapter mentioned one-arm traversing as a tool for developing dynamic technique. It also provides excellent power-endurance training.

One-arm traverses require a wall (preferably vertical) with holds at least one digit's width. Traverse it as long as you can, then switch hands. In addition to promoting forearm power-endurance in situations of severely restricted blood flow, this exercise promotes contact strength since

catching each hold requires a momentary extra burst of strength.

Be wary of this exercise if you have a history of shoulder or finger problems. If one-arm traverses are too intense, try using both arms together as if they were one. Dyno both hands at once from hold to hold.

Anaerobic Training on Fingerboards

Because of the importance of specificity in local anaerobic training, it's important that fingerboard training be done in a way that simulates the demands climbing places on the finger and forearm muscles.

Intensive Power-endurance Training on Fingerboard	
Load	60–75%
Duration of hang	To failure (should be 25–40 seconds)
Rest between sets	45–60 seconds
Sets	12–15

Extensive Power-endurance Training on Fingerboard	
Load	50%
Duration of hang	To failure (should be 45–60 seconds)
Rest between sets	60–90 seconds
Sets	15–30

As with other types of fingerboard training, these routines should be done using both static continuous hangs and static-intermittent hangs, in which weight shifts from hand to hand.

Anaerobic Training off the Wall

The importance of specificity in anaerobic training makes it vital to use methods that replicate the situations you're training for. For this reason, we don't recommend anaerobic training using grippers, weights, or any other devices that don't accurately simulate climbing.

If you don't work exactly the right muscles in the same positions and directions of force they'll need for the types of climbing you're training for, you may reap very little benefit and risk decreasing your performance because of the ease of anaerobic overtraining.

Other Aspects of Anaerobic Training

Although local anaerobic training is one of the most common forms of training among climbers, it is easily abused. Because of its sustained use of high power in the toxic presence of lactic acid, local anaerobic training has a high potential for overtraining and must be undertaken with caution.

High concentrations of lactic acid hurt for good reason. The pain-causing acidity can kill mitochondria, the aerobic restorers of ATP. High-volume anaerobic training thus decreases muscles' aerobic abilities. As we saw in the last chapter (see Trade-offs), it also can lower maximum recruitment.

Fortunately, anaerobic processes respond quickly to training, so relatively brief training phases are necessary. If the other aspects of strength are developed, anaerobic training can be used intermittently to bring overall performance to a peak.

Unfortunately, climbing single-pitch routes at one's limit often pushes local anaerobic systems to their limit. This suggests that sport climbing is inherently susceptible to overtraining. So it's very

The role of power-endurance in sport climbing makes it susceptible to overtraining. Jim Karn in competition at the 1991 World Championships in Frankfurt, Germany.

important to have times during the year when you concentrate on bouldering, climb longer and easier routes, or rest altogether. It also suggests that periodization (the sequencing of different periods of training emphasis) is especially crucial to maximizing performance in our sport.

Aerobic Energy Restoration and Capillarity (ARC)

Training the muscles' anaerobic systems involves loads high enough to restrict blood flow to the muscles. Taxing their aerobic capacities, on the other hand, requires that muscles have access to blood. Training the local aerobic capacity thus involves lighter loads on the muscles being used. By sustaining this lighter intensity for a longer duration, the aerobic components within the muscles adapt to high demands for aerobic energy restoration.

Conveniently, capillarity is fostered under the same training conditions. Since capillarity improvements result from raised blood pressure against the tiny capillary walls, training to develop it requires sustained muscle use at intensities low enough to keep all capillaries open. Uninterrupted use for thirty to forty-five minutes at constant loads best promotes capillarity.

The optimal load for developing aerobic restoration and capillarity, or ARC, is around 30 percent of maximum strength. At this intensity you should feel a very mild but not painful pump that you can climb with indefinitely. The burning pump that characterizes strenuous endurance routes squeezes capillaries shut—the opposite of what you want. The presence of lactic acid reduces the quantity of ARC training you can accommodate, and training in thirty- to forty-five-minute sessions relies on quantity.

When you're finished, your arms should feel used, warm, and full of blood, but not tight or hard. They should feel almost the same near the end of the workout as they did ten minutes into it.

Aerobic Restoration and Capillarity Training Overview

Load	20–35%
Duration	30–45 minutes
Sets	1–2
Rest between sets	Half an hour or more
Should feel	Like you're not doing it hard enough
Recovery time	If you're not recovered in 18 hours, your load was too high
Phase length	Can do indefinitely

ARC Training through Climbing

To train ARC by climbing, you need to climb continuously for at least half an hour. You can pause in rest positions while climbing, but choose terrain that's easy enough that you don't have to stop and recover. Try to keep the intensity consistent throughout the session.

ARC sessions are a good opportunity to work on other aspects of your climbing. Since you're climbing at far from 100 percent intensity, you can spare the awareness to think about new techniques you want to try, or work on fluid breathing or other forms of relaxation. Thirty-minute sessions also raise your level of composure and comfort during extended pitches.

■ **On Routes.** In choosing a route for this type of training, it's best to err on the easy side. Falling off as soon as you get pumped on a route that's slightly too hard means your muscles have gone anaerobic and you've contributed nothing toward ARC. On a route that's slightly too easy, however,

Thirty-minute climbing sessions improve your comfort and composure on long pitches.

there are many things you can do to increase the difficulty. You can climb more quickly or avoid rests and large holds. You can even contrive more difficult sequences or do lock-off training (see Technique Training: Practice, chapter 4).

Down-climb routes to avoid having to lower off. Since we're more adept at climbing up than down, seek clusters of routes where you can climb up one, then down an easier one. Remember that they'll have to be way below your limit for you to climb continuously.

Gyms are perfect for ARC training. Look for a top-rope covering several routes in your range. If you have to change ropes to a different top-rope, don't worry about a few

seconds off the wall. Just try to minimize any "down time."

■ **Bouldering.** You can avoid boring your belayers by ARC training while bouldering. Just remember that you're after a steady, continuous level of relatively easy climbing. A traverse where you can do many moves without getting too high off the deck is best.

This is often easiest to find on artificial walls or buildings. If you're climbing on a hold-studded wall, you can try climbing with particular themes for part of your session. A half-hour spent working on back-stepping, twist-locking, or doing moderate cross-through moves reveals many subtleties of each technique. If you're doing it with a forearms and more closely simulates climbing than static hanging.

The biggest obstacle to ARC training on fingerboards is boredom. Half an hour is a long time to spend on so few holds. Listening to a Walkman, talking to friends, or doing psychological exercises of a set duration can help.

ARC Training off the Wall

For those who can't train on holds, some "squeezing" devices can help your aerobic system. This has the advantage of being possible while doing a wide variety of other activities. Just remember that because gripping these devices is never exactly like holding onto holds, the transfer of training improvements to your climbing will never be as high as when the training is climbing-specific.

Again, the object is to develop a slight pump and hold it for at least thirty minutes. If you feel your forearms burning, you're doing it too hard.

Other Aspects of ARC Training

Because of its low intensity and tendency to flush the muscles with blood, ARC training promotes athletic and even injury recovery if done carefully. Just realize that the boundary between local aerobic and anaerobic training is narrow.

Aspects of strength that arise from physical changes in the muscles, like capillarity, require the longest time to be developed. We'll say more about this in the Periodization chapter, but for now, know that ARC training is valuable throughout your climbing and training seasons.

Ideally, you could finish your climbing days with easy thirty-minute climbing sessions. This not only flushes out waste

Bouldering walls with long traverses are ideal for solitary thirty-minute sessions. Udo Neumann on the Great Wall of China.

partner, the stick game (see chapter 4) can help pass the time more quickly.

ARC Training on Fingerboards

For the motivated, ARC training can be done on fingerboards. Staying on for thirty minutes will require standing in elastic bands to reduce your body weight (surgical tubing or bike inner tubes also work). Move your hands from hold to hold to involve the full spectrum of holds offered by your fingerboard. This helps move blood through your products accumulated during the day but also takes you a step further in the gradual development of capillarity.

LONG-TERM STRENGTH DEVELOPMENT

At thirty-something, Bruno's nervous. "I've been training for years. Can I still get stronger?" Research on weight lifters of the former Soviet Union suggests that significant improvement is possible even after ten years of hard training and in athletes over the age of thirty-five. According to Soviet scientists, strength gains are more the result of nerve-related changes, such as those responsible for increasing the recruitment of fibers, than biochemical or physical adaptations. In addition, bones and other structures must adapt to the stimulus of training for strength gains to occur. Studies on osteoporosis show that training continues to have these effects at any age.

Summary of Strength Training			
Muscular quality	Goal	Training it requires	Notes
Intermuscular coordination	Balanced development of the muscles used in climbing	Using muscles exactly as they are used in climbing	Most of the time, climbing is the best training for climbing
Hypertrophy	Size increase	Exercises emphasizing the same muscle group for 4–10 repetitions or 6–15 seconds	Weight training produces the fastest hypertrophy gains but does nothing for technique
Maximum recruitment	Ability to recruit the maximum number of fibers	Very brief maximum-intensity efforts	Must be properly periodized for best results
Anaerobic metabolism	Ability to produce energy via anaerobic pathway	Efforts of an intensity and duration that produce a burning pump	Specificity is crucial; susceptible to overtraining
Aerobic restoration and capillarity	Ability to produce energy via aerobic pathway; increased density of blood vessels within the muscles	Easy 30–45-minute uninterrupted climbing sessions	A low-intensity training mode that enhances recovery as a bonus

11. GENERAL ENDURANCE

Think what it's like to run at a moderate pace on flat terrain. No individual muscles suffer from oxygen starvation or lactic overload. Instead, the whole-body systems that support muscular work are taxed—specifically, the heart, lungs, and blood supply network, or *cardiovascular system*. Working muscles require sustenance from the rest of your body. They need oxygen and nutrients delivered to them, and they need their wastes removed. Taking care of this for a few smaller muscles is easy, but when several larger muscles demand these services simultaneously, it adds up to a large task for the organs responsible.

General endurance refers to the stamina of the systems (the heart and lungs) that support muscular work wherever it occurs in the body; local endurance refers to the capacity of individual muscles to do sustained work.

When many muscles are active at once, the cardiovascular system can become the limiting factor in performance. The heart can only pump so fast; the lungs can only take in so much air. Whereas local endurance reflects abilities and qualities within individual muscles, general endurance refers to the ability of these central organs to support athletic work. When only a few muscles are actively working, the cardiovascular system meets athletic demands at its normal level of operation. But when more than about 20 percent of your total muscle mass is working, it must increase its operating rate to keep up. Its ability to do this determines the body's level of general endurance.

To decide if general endurance training is appropriate in your training, consider its role in climbing, recovery, fat loss, and countering the effects of stress.

IS GENERAL ENDURANCE IMPORTANT IN CLIMBING?

Since hardly any climbing situation, even a rest position, demands work from less than 20 percent of your total muscle mass, general endurance is clearly involved in climbing. Whether or not general endurance training will directly increase climbing ability, however, hinges on whether general endurance is a limiting factor in climbing.

To answer this question, let's compare climbing with other classic general endurance sports. Do athletes in general endurance sports experience the same physiological changes as climbers do?

Although climbing performances can last from a few seconds (bouldering) to more than thirty minutes (long, sustained pitches), most sport climbs take three to fifteen minutes to complete. Athletes in rowing events of a comparable duration, or in the fifteen-hundred-meter run, show extremely high lactic acid concentrations (20 mmol in a liter of blood), and their pulse rates reach 210 beats per minute. Comparing these figures to those of climbers at their limits reveals a big contrast.

Tests at the German Sports Institute in Cologne showed that most sport climbs are far from producing high endurance data. Climbers on difficult on-sights exhibited maximum lactic acid concentrations of only 8 mmol per liter[1] and heart rates of just 180 beats per minute. If expert climbers rate an effort as very difficult when it shows only moderate numbers in these measurements, it reveals that general endurance rarely limits rock climbing performance.

The fact that climbers' data are lower than those of general endurance athletes doesn't mean that climbing isn't as difficult as running or rowing. Instead, it points to the nature of climbing's challenge.

First, *local* endurance, not general endurance, is the limiting stamina factor for climbers. Individual muscles are pushed to their limits, but the body as a whole doesn't approach its limits of energy production.

Second, climbing is extremely coordination dependent. Remember from chapter 2 how lactic acid cripples coordination? If coordination were less critical to climbing, higher lactic acid levels could be tolerated before climbers failed. But as it is, bloodstream lactic acid levels that exceed a relatively low threshold impair coordination enough to cause climbers to fall off. Climbing's coordination dependence prevents it from being a sport that pushes general endurance near its limits.

Bruno protests, "But on difficult pitches, my heart races, I gasp for breath, and my lactic acid levels are higher than those I've felt in any other activity!"

First let's address his lactic acid claim. Lactic concentrations do get sky-high, but only at a local level as a result of extreme use of comparatively small muscles. Bloodstream levels never reach impressive heights. The problem in climbing is getting lactic acid out of the muscle and into the bloodstream.

Heavy breathing during difficult climbs can result from use of the abdominal muscles: in difficult positions, it's impossible to maintain body tension and breathe at the same time. Psychological tension and insecurity also make people suspend breathing temporarily, only to breathe hard to repay their oxygen debt once they resume.

---

[1] *Unlike those of other endurance athletes, lactic acid levels in climbers' bloodstreams peak several minutes after finishing a climb. This results from the difficulty of removing lactic acid from continuously contracted muscles, like the forearms, until after they relax.*

Finally, why does Bruno's heart race? The contraction of abdominal muscles during high-body-tension climbing raises blood pressure. This makes the heart take quicker, shallower beats. Climbers' rapid heart rates reflect temporary high blood pressure, not the extreme demands for blood that characterize general endurance activities.

So why isn't general endurance a weak link in climbing? Because most climbing routes don't require the cyclic movements of large muscle groups that classic endurance sports involve. Climbing works many large muscles at moderate capacity, but it only works a few small muscles to their absolute limit. As a result, the heart and lungs are not overburdened by muscular demands.

Since general endurance is not a weak link in climbing, training it won't improve your climbing directly, as other forms of training aim to do. Going on strenuous runs is likely to give a climber nothing more than something extra to recover from.

However, *low-intensity* general endurance training does have significant effects on some of the peripheral issues climbers face. When general endurance exercise is done *aerobically*, it aids climbers struggling with fat loss, athletic recovery, and stress.

GENERAL AEROBIC ENDURANCE TRAINING AND FAT LOSS

Since body weight is important in climbing, fat loss is a near obsession with many climbers. Although the fat fixation is often unjustified, some people could stand to shed some fat. Unfortunately, most of the popular approaches to fat loss have little or no effect on body fat levels. Here we'll consider the role of general aerobic endurance training (GAET) in fat loss.

The idea behind losing fat is basic: you must burn more calories than you consume. In reality, however, people fight more than simple mathematics. Along with genetic programming that determines hair color, size, and physical makeup come predetermined guidelines for how much fat to maintain. These guidelines are set differently for each person.

Your body holds your body fat at its guideline, or "set-point," level by adjusting your metabolism and hunger. When your body fat is above your set-point, for example, your hunger decreases and your metabolism speeds up; body fat naturally decreases as a result. When your fat level drops below your body's desired level, your metabolism slows and your appetite picks up, making it easier to gain fat and harder to lose it.

Although you can fight your set-point, it's impossible to eliminate its influence, because its control of your desire to eat is much stronger than your will power. It works nonstop to make your body want to achieve its goal. Unless you can alter the set-point, you're fighting a losing battle.

Research shows no link between diet and this set-point. It does, however, suggest a link between GAET and the fat set-point. By habituating the body to burning fat for fuel, GAET makes it easier for the body to tap its fat reserves. The body's ability to burn fat is partly a question of physiological habit. When people avoid fat-burning situations by going from snack to snack and never doing aerobic exercise, their bodies rarely *have* to burn fat. Such people have a harder time switching to fat-burning mode. Developing a physiological habit of fat burning may be part of how GAET lowers the body fat set-point.

GAET is thus a multipronged attack on fat. First, it burns more fat than any other kind of exercise while you're doing it. Second, it tips the caloric balance in your favor. Most significantly, over the long term, it can act to lower the body's fat set-point.

Since it requires a state of caloric deficiency, lowering body fat negatively affects many other types of training. It can be unhealthy for those for whom it isn't a valid need.

GAET AND ATHLETIC RECOVERY

In Physical Training Principles we discussed the crucial role of the recovery period separating workouts. Without it, physical improvement is impossible. To a large extent, the muscles' access to blood determines the rate of athletic recovery because blood carries the oxygen and nutrients necessary for repair.

The circulation of blood throughout the body is partly determined by muscle use. Unfortunately, the sedentary lifestyle most people lead between workouts does little to promote active blood circulation. If you spend most of your days sitting, your body has no reason to maintain high

circulation to your muscles. Psychological stress also reduces blood flow to the extremities (as a safety mechanism to reduce blood loss during injury). Consequently, many athletes recover much more slowly than they could.

Enter general endurance. GAET opens up blood vessels and increases circulation throughout the body, both during exercise and for several hours following it. It does so without adding much physical stress for the body to recover from. In addition, as we'll see in a moment, it reduces the effects of psychological stress. As a result, GAET between workouts speeds athletic recovery.

GAET AND STRESS

Stress is more than just a feeling. It's a "wear and tear" effect that results from an excess of demands on your mind and body. It leads to poor athletic recovery and reduced immunity to illness.

Stress, both physical and mental, keeps the body in an aroused, performance-oriented state. Yet athletic recovery is optimized in the chemical climates characteristic of more relaxed states. Healthy athletic improvement requires a balance of the two. The stress state provides the stimulus for supercompensation and adaptation; the relaxed recovery state provides the condition in which recovery and supercompensation can occur.

Many people in today's world live with an excess of the stress state and a shortage of the recovery state. After a caffeine-fueled nine hours in a stressful job setting, Bruno battles traffic on the way to the gym to lift weights. Then he hurries home to a quick dinner before watching a horror movie on video.

The stress of the modern lifestyle is attributable to the summed effects of the stressors we face. Bruno is physically or emotionally overexcited at all times. Unfortunately, this adrenalin lifestyle wreaks havoc on athletic recovery, because stress fatigues the mechanisms that fuel recovery in the body. When prolonged, stress becomes a form of hormonal "injury." This is where GAET comes in.

Anaerobic exercise, like weight lifting and most climbing, produces many of the same hormones associated with psychological stress. As a result, it contributes to the effects of other stressors in one's life. Aerobic exercise, on the other hand, increases hormones associated with the recovery state. Thus aerobic general endurance activities oppose and reduce the effects of stress, so adding them to your training can increase the amount of *anaerobic* training your body can healthily accommodate. Whereas a weight training program compounds stress, adding GAET to a stressful lifestyle reduces it. GAET can help restore a healthy balance of stress and recovery to an overly stressful life.

CONCLUSIONS

This book aims to help you improve at climbing. This goal prioritizes our focus on activities that are the weakest links in the chain of abilities climbing involves. General endurance itself is not a weak link in your climbing and thus is unlikely to improve your ability directly. Low-intensity general endurance exercise can, however, help you deal with other factors that may be weak links in your climbing.

- If losing fat is a priority (it's not for most climbers), GAET is an essential part of doing so.
- If you have plenty of time to devote to training and recovery is a limiting factor in your improvement rate, it can speed your improvement.
- If you have an excess of nonphysical stress in your life, GAET can reduce the physiological consequences your body suffers.

Reaping these benefits requires a particular approach to general endurance training. In the next chapter, we'll examine how to go about it.

12. GENERAL ENDURANCE TRAINING

WHAT LEVEL OF INTENSITY SHOULD I USE?

Since general endurance isn't a limiting factor in our sport, climbers needn't focus on drastically improving their general endurance capacities. They have enough skills and abilities to improve at already. Applying a high level of general endurance stress to their bodies would only give them an unnecessary burden to recover from.

As we hinted in the last chapter, the benefits general endurance training offers climbers (fat loss, recovery, and stress relief) occur at an intensity in which the body meets its energy needs aerobically. We called this general aerobic endurance training, or GAET. In fact, these benefits are all sacrificed at the higher intensities that general endurance athletes often use in their training.

Just as the presence of oxygen in an individual muscle affects whether it produces its energy aerobically or anaerobically, oxygen availability in the body determines how muscle groups involved in general endurance activities produce their energy. Keeping your general endurance training aerobic requires not exceeding a certain intensity of exercise.

The easiest way to regulate the intensity of general endurance work is by monitoring your heart rate. The figure on the next page shows the heart rates that are appropriate for the different aims discussed in this and the previous chapter. When doing GAET,

check your heart rate periodically to confirm that you are within your target range.

If you don't want to spend $100 or more for a heart rate monitor, just count your pulse periodically for a six-second period and multiply by ten to calculate your beats per minute. At first you'll have to measure your heart rate periodically to get an idea of what the desired intensity feels like. Eventually, you'll learn the "feel" of your target zone.

Many climbers are surprised to learn how easy an aerobic intensity is. Too many believe that beneficial training should hurt, or at least feel difficult. GAET doesn't. At the proper intensity, you should be able to maintain a conversation easily. If running, you should be able to take at least three steps for each inhale or exhale. Going harder only *sacrifices* the benefits GAET offers. When you finish you should be limbered up but by no means worn out.

And though the intensity of GAET is only moderate, take the time for a warm-up and cool-down. You should reach your target zone only after five minutes or more of gradually increasing the intensity of your chosen activity.

WHAT TYPE OF EXERCISE SHOULD I DO?

Many general endurance exercises, like running, rope skipping, swimming, and biking, can be done almost anywhere. Others, like rowing and nordic skiing, may require specific conditions or equipment.

●–Target heart rates (beats per minute) for different ages and training goals*–●

Age	Maximum heart rate	85% of maximum	75% of maximum	65% of maximum
15	205	174	153	133
20	200	170	150	130
25	195	166	146	127
30	190	162	143	124
35	185	157	139	120
45	175	149	131	114
55	165	140	124	107
65	155	132	116	101
75	145	123	109	94

Serious general endurance conditioning range (inappropriate for climbers' training)

Stress reduction range: 15 minutes or longer (as needed)

Fat burning range: 40 minutes or more (before breakfast best)

Athletic recovery range: 20-30 minutes (best after workouts or on rest days)

* Subtract 15 beats per minute to find your target rate for swimming.

To work the cardiovascular system, general endurance exercise spreads athletic workload over a large quantity of muscle mass. That way no individual muscles are pushed near their local endurance limits. Many general endurance sports do this by focusing on the large muscles of the legs. If the smaller upper body muscles are emphasized, they must typically be combined with lower body muscles to achieve a high enough muscle mass to distribute the exercise load.

The muscles your chosen general endurance workout involves will have little consequence on the hormonal or cardiovascular benefits of GAET, or on the location of fat burned. Thus one form of it will be as effective as another for stress relief or fat burning. But your choice of exercises *will* impact the recovery effects you experience. Upper body GAET like swimming, rowing, or nordic skiing flushes the upper body's muscles more effectively than running or biking. More important, using upper body muscles continuously for thirty minutes or more helps develop their capillarity, promoting quicker recovery even during times of inactivity.

GAET for Athletic Recovery

To decide whether GAET would help your recovery, consider your training volume. For Bruno, who trains three times a week, recovery rate is not a significant factor. Since he has at least one rest day between every training day and he alternates between different workouts, he is usually recovered from his last workout before he begins the next. Therefore, speeding up his recovery time wouldn't speed his improvement.

For Max, however, recovery rate is a big issue. In his quest for the top grades, Max would gladly train every day if his body could take it. As it is he grudgingly takes rest days because he has learned the hard way that he gets worse, not better, if he trains every day.

For him, low-intensity aerobic exercise following his heavy workouts speeds his recovery, shortening recovery periods between workouts. It also helps him reduce muscle soreness and stiffness the morning after hard workouts. Adding general endurance training increases the amount of athletic stimulus his body can adapt to. As a result, Max takes an easy half-hour jog or swim three times a week.

GAET for Fat Loss

Burning fat for fuel requires more oxygen than does burning glycogen. Consequently, if oxygen is scarce, your body reduces fat burning to conserve it. Running anaerobically, therefore, burns very little fat.

So if your muscles burn from lactic acid or you're gasping for air, you know you're not burning fat. A moderate, steady pace is best for fat burning. For example, a moderate pace in running means six to eight steps per full breath cycle. And since fat use begins slowly and increases gradually after starting a workout, you must exercise at least thirty-five minutes to get a significant fat-burning effect.

The timing of your endurance exercise also affects the amount of fat it burns. If you run within a few hours of eating, the steady supply of calories from your digesting food will take the place of calories that would otherwise have come from stored fat. By contrast, after a night of sleep, your body is already in fat-burning mode, so general endurance exercise at this time burns a maximum amount of fat.

Remember, however, that significant fat loss is incompatible with many types of training.

GAET for Stress Relief

GAET of a comparable or even lower intensity than that for enhancing recovery and fat burning shows positive effects in reducing stress. Other factors, however, will contribute to or detract from effective stress reduction. Your best chance at success comes by combining other known stress killers with your exercise. Make your GAET sessions fun and playful. Let them expose you to natural beauty. Vary the workout from one session to the next. If you feel like you have to do it, don't.

13. FLEXIBILITY

Flexibility refers to the range of possible movement around a joint or a sequence of joints that a person can access. A climber's flexibility determines the body positions he may use and can be a limiting factor in his movement efficiency on rock.

Climbers need flexibility for:

- High-stepping, crossovers with the arms, stemming, reaching over roofs, and so on
- Optimally positioning the center of gravity close to the rock in vertical climbing
- Efficient use of rest positions
- Preventing injuries.

To illustrate flexibility's value in climbing situations, consider the men's 1989 Nürnburg World Cup. Britain's Jerry Moffat and Japan's Yuji Hirayama both had a good shot at first place. But Yuji's superior flexibility won him the competition despite Jerry's incomparable finger strength.

Note in the video prints on page 134 that as Jerry pulled over the roof (photos A & B), he struggled to get his feet onto the vertical wall. Unable to stay close to the wall for a rest, he was forced to continue upward with tired arms, and he fell a few moves later.

When Yuji reached this sequence, his greater flexibility allowed him to keep his body lower and closer to the wall as he brought his final foot above the lip. This improved his direction of pull on the handholds, since he was pulling more downward on his holds (E) than Jerry had (B). Once he stood up on the footholds, Yuji's flexibility even allowed him to shake off some of the roof's pump (F) before moving on to flash the route and win the competition.

PASSIVE FLEXIBILITY

The limits of a joint's range of motion depend on the joint's construction, the ligaments surrounding it, and the length of

Julia stretching.

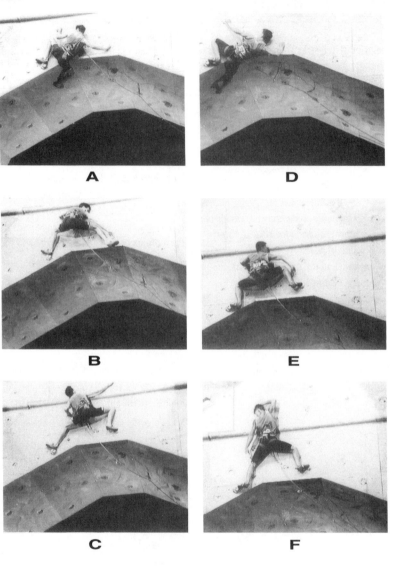

A

D

B

E

C

F

the tendons and muscles attaching across it. Since you can't change the joint, bones, ligaments, or tendons, the only way to increase a joint's passive range of motion (the range it can access with external help) is by *lengthening muscles* through stretching.

Remember from the Coordination chapter that any stretch or contraction is monitored by a muscle's spindles. When you stretch a muscle too hard or too unsteadily, a safety mechanism of the spindles called the stretch reflex signals the muscle to contract. This tightens the muscle to prevent further lengthening, and it generally hurts.

On the bright side, this reflex helps prevent damage caused by unexpected movements beyond a muscle's safe range of motion. Unfortunately, it also prevents most people from effectively stretching their muscles.

To enhance flexibility, stretching must first overcome the stretch reflex. In the next chapter we'll discuss two stretching techniques that do.

ACTIVE FLEXIBILITY

Being able to use our full range of motion depends on more than simple muscle length. When most people stretch, they use gravity and external aid to force their limbs into the difficult positions at the limits of their passive flexibility. But in real climbing situations, we can't force our limbs into stretched positions. We must pull them into those positions using our own muscle power.

Active flexibility refers to the range of motion a limb or body part can access using its own muscle strength. How high, for example, can you lift your leg for a high-step without leaning backward? For climbers, active flexibility is the more important type of flexibility to achieve.

Since active flexibility relies on the body's own muscles to pull a limb into position, the flexibility of a muscle is no less important than the strength of the antagonist muscles that oppose it. In addition, our muscles'

strength is specific to the *positions* in which we develop them. A muscle that's strong in its customary ranges of use can be weak in extreme positions that are infrequently used. Normal strengthening techniques therefore don't guarantee good active flexibility. For passive flexibility gains to be useful on the rock, they must be accompanied by exercises to build antagonist strength in these new ranges of motion that stretching opens up.

GENDER PRIORITIES

Women typically have better passive flexibility than men. But males' higher natural recruitment gives them more power to pull their less flexible limbs into extreme positions. As a result, gender differences in active flexibility aren't as pronounced as those in passive flexibility.

This means that men can profitably spend a higher percentage of their flexibility training working on passive flexibility, whereas women typically need to spend more time addressing their active flexibility.

PAIN AND STRETCHING

To stretch safely and effectively, each athlete must learn about the sensations that characterize stretching. Constructive stretching can pull uncomfortably on muscles, but many athletes learn to enjoy this feeling.

A threshold of pain exists beyond which damage occurs in a stretched muscle. When pulled to this extent, microtears develop that shorten the muscle when it repairs. Extreme overstretching causes scar tissue formation, making future lengthening of the muscle more difficult. When stretching starts to hurt, *back off!*

KEEPING A BALANCE

Flexibility can be a deciding factor in overall fitness for climbing. Indeed, you can hardly be too flexible in your legs. It's important, however, to keep your focus in balance. Overemphasizing flexibility in your training exposes you to the same pitfalls as overemphasis of other physical abilities. Just as overdeveloped lock-off strength can lead to an inefficiently static style of climbing, an obsession with turnout flexibility can lead a climber to overuse positions involving flexibility when better options exist. The stretching fanatic's dedication to climbing flexibly makes him less prone to an extended tiptoe or drop-knee move that may require no flexibility at all.

Climbing styles evolve like fashions, and flexibility is an integral part of a climbing style. Climbers who overuse the frog position typically started climbing in the early 1980s when the great frog, Patrick Edlinger, and others helped convince climbers that flexibility was important. As climbers have learned to use the outside edges of their shoes and drop-knee techniques, turnout flexibility has become less crucial to a good climbing style. And for those with less than perfect turnout, climbing tall often takes more weight off their arms.

So don't get into a rut. Don't let flexibility take up more than 15 percent of your training time, and don't dedicate all your flexibility training to just one or two "show" stretches. In the training chapter that follows we'll look at how to improve flexibility throughout your body.

14. FLEXIBILITY TRAINING

To show you how to become more limber, we'll consider approaches to increasing flexibility. These are principles you can apply regardless of the particular position or stretch you perform. We'll also focus on specific stretching positions to increase your range of motion in different parts of your body and target the muscles involved.

WARMING UP FOR STRETCHING

Cold muscles respond poorly to stretching and injure easily at an intensity that could be beneficial if they were warm. Be sure to do a full warm-up (see chapter 8, Physical Training Principles) before starting any serious stretching.

The range-of-motion exercises described in chapter 8 are good exercises to do before stretching in earnest, even if your muscles are already warm. They lightly stretch muscles, warming and preparing them for activity or for more serious stretching. And though they are primarily warm-up exercises, even alone they can increase flexibility in muscles that normally never move through their full ranges of motion.

As we mentioned before in describing effective warm-up techniques, *light* stretching before a climb can help loosen and prepare muscles for activity. But the best time to work on developing flexibility through stretching is after climbing or working out. With your muscles thoroughly warmed up, they are most responsive to flexibility training.

Avoid hard stretching before demanding climbs. Stretching stresses the muscle spindles, interfering with their ability to relay precise information on body or limb positioning. Thus hard stretching before climbing can interfere with a climber's kinesthetic senses.

HOW TO STRETCH

As we've discussed, the goal of stretching is to lengthen the muscle beyond its normal limit without spurring the inhibiting stretch reflex. The following two methods accomplish this.

Slow, Steady Stretching (SSS)

The simplest effective stretching technique is slow, steady stretching, which increases muscle length very gradually. When muscle spindles don't sense the danger that sudden movements pose, they suspend their stretch reflex and allow the muscle to be lengthened beyond its normal length.

After assuming a stretch position, gradually lengthen the muscle over a period of ten to fifteen seconds, stopping further lengthening before the stretch becomes painful. Hold it at this maximum length for fifteen seconds. Let the muscle rest for a minute or so, then repeat the process one or two more times.

Contract, Hold, Relax, Stretch (CHRS)

CHRS is a sequence of contractions and relaxations that desensitizes the muscle-tendon unit and prevents the stretch reflex. To do a CHRS stretch, assume a position in which the muscle is just beginning to be stretched.

- Contract the stretched muscle tightly without moving the limb (this is called an isometric contraction). For example, if you're stretching in the "splits" position, you'd try to squeeze your legs back together again.
- Hold the contraction for five to eight seconds.
- Relax *suddenly.*
- Stretch the muscle steadily just beyond its former limit for ten seconds or more.

Repeat this sequence two to four times for the best stretch.

Both CHRS and SSS are unstressful forms of physical training that you can easily do almost anywhere. Although it's best to stay mentally "with" any form of training, you can stretch while conversing or reading and still know that you've done something to improve your climbing.

Remember, however, that stretching only covers the passive aspect of flexibility. For many muscles, that's only half the equation.

Active Range of Movement (ARM)

The following exercise helps develop the strength to use the new ranges of motion that stretching opens up, and it narrows the gap between your passive and active flexibility. It's easiest to do with a partner, but it can be done alone too.

The exercise consists of pulling into a passive stretch, then releasing whatever external aid helped to achieve that position. Upon releasing, you attempt to maintain the stretched position under the power of the muscles in that limb or area. Depending on your positioning, gravity will either enhance or decrease the difficulty of actively holding the stretched position.

To try it, stand facing a partner. Allow your partner to lift one of your legs up in front of you. Bend at the hip and keep your leg straight at the knee. Once it's high enough to stretch the hamstring muscles on the back of your thigh, have your partner release your leg, and try to maintain its height under your own power. The amount it drops reflects the deficit between your active and passive flexibility. Repeat this process three to five times for effective ARM training.

Ideally, ARM exercises should be done immediately following passive stretches so that strength is built in the fullest possible range of motion.

The need for ARM exercises is not uniform throughout the body. In the lower body, using one's full active flexibility involves overcoming not only the tension of the muscles being stretched but also the weight of lifting a large limb (and shoe) against the force of gravity. So after lengthening muscles like the hamstrings, you should strengthen their antagonists to develop active flexibility for climbing situations.

It's a different story with the upper body. Lighter limbs and smaller muscles make it easier to achieve full active flexibility. ARM exercises are typically unnecessary for upper body flexibility.

WHAT TO STRETCH IN YOUR LOWER BODY

The hip area most directly influences climbing-specific flexibility in the legs. The critical muscles there include:

- The adductor muscle group. These muscles lie along the inside of the thighs and act to pull the legs together. Stretching them improves the legs' range of motion in the side-split and turnout positions.
- The hamstring muscles. They run from the knee to the buttocks along the underside of the thighs. They're stretched when you bend over to touch your toes. Hamstring flexibility improves high-step ability, especially for holds a few feet away from you or in stemming positions.
- The gluteal muscles. These are large, powerful muscles that pull the thigh downward and help pull the legs open into stem positions. Stretching them improves high-step ability for holds close in front of the body.
- The iliopsoas muscles. They run from the lower spine through the abdomen to the thigh; they act to lift the leg upward. Tight iliopsoas muscles make it hard to arch backward at the hip joint or to lean the upper body backward while the thigh remains parallel to a vertical wall.

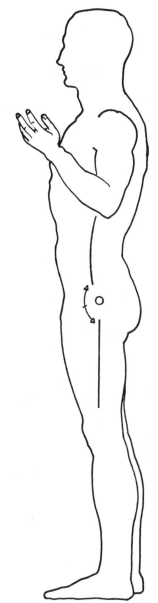

Tight iliopsoas muscles inhibit straightening of the leg at the hip joint.

To optimally develop flexibility in each of these groups, use the following four-step method. We'll describe it first in general terms, then go over it again for each of the critical muscle groups listed above.

1. After a warm-up, begin by swinging or moving the muscles you'll stretch through their full ranges of motion for fifteen to twenty seconds.
2. Begin stretching via the slow, steady stretching method. Hold each stretch for twenty to thirty seconds, and stretch each leg one to three times. Stretch your muscles to what feels like 80 percent of a maximum healthy intensity.
3. Next use CHRS to maximize your stretching stimulus. This can be done in the same positions as the SSS you've just finished doing. Perform each cycle of contraction and relaxation two to four times for each muscle you stretch.
4. Now that your muscles are well stretched, do ARM exercises to build strength in the new ranges of motion you've opened up.

To see how this four-step sequence works on the critical muscle groups we described, follow along with the illustrations. We begin with the adductor muscle group.

Start by gently thrusting the leg to the side for ten to twenty seconds (Photo 1). Then assume positions from which you can do slow, steady stretching and CHRS stretching. Photos 2, 3, and 4 give examples of some stretches that target the adductor muscles.

With these muscles well stretched, do ARM exercises to build strength in the new

1

2

3

ranges of motion you've opened up. This can be done by grasping and releasing your knee and lifting your bent leg to the

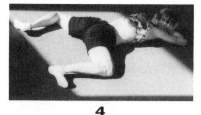

4

6

5

· **7**

side until you feel a stretch (5). Abruptly release your leg with your hand, trying to maintain the same position under your leg's own power (6). For those with exceptional flexibility, a similar ARM sequence is achieved by grasping the foot instead of the knee (7 and 8).

For the hamstrings, begin by swinging each leg forward toward its flexibility limit for ten to twenty seconds (9). Then take a position in which you can do SSS of the hamstrings, like that in Photo 10. Next, do

142

8

10

9

11

CHRS by trying to straighten your stretched legs at the hip. Do CHRS either in a seated position on the floor or leaning against a support so that your torso is upright (11).

12

14

13

15

Finally, do ARM exercises in a comparable fashion to those you just did for your adductor muscles (12 and 13).

The gluteal muscles are hard to stretch via swinging motions. A better alternative for a gluteal warm-up stretch is shown in Photo 14. This also makes a good stretch for the muscles of the lower spine. Next take a position from which you can do slow, steady stretches (15 and 16) and CHRS. To do ARM exercises for these muscles, assume a standing position and hold your ankle in front of you with your knee to the side, in an orientation resembling that in Photo 16. Release your ankle and attempt to maintain

16

17

flexibility series for the hip region and works both the passive and active aspects of stretching. With a little imagination you can apply the same four-step series to a variety of other positions and motions.

WHAT TO STRETCH IN YOUR UPPER BODY

We've discussed why ARM exercises are unnecessary for upper body muscles. Developing healthy, performance-enhancing flexibility in your upper body muscles is simply a matter of learning a few basic positions and stealing moments between efforts in climbing and training for some SSS and CHRS stretches. These stretches are important even if you are already happy with your current upper body flexibility, because without stretching, muscles shorten as they recover from the exercises that strengthen them.

Critical areas for upper body flexibility include the arms, shoulders, and upper spine. Be careful in working with these smaller muscles. They require less force to achieve a stretch than do the larger muscles of the lower body and are more easily over-stretched.

Photo 18 stretches the triceps, shoulders, and upper spine. Move the body gently

your foot's former position using your own leg power.

For the iliopsoas muscles, thrust your leg in a gentle swinging motion backward for ten to twenty seconds. Photo 17 shows a position that stretches the iliopsoas muscles. When using this stretch, emphasize these muscles by keeping your spine upright while pressing your buttocks toward the floor. Iliopsoas ARM exercises are not necessary for the positions climbing requires.

Applying this four-step sequence to these four muscle groups provides a complete

18

backward and toward the floor while your straightened arm remains parked at the same point on the floor. This can also be done standing as you lean a straightened arm against a wall.

Photo 19 stretches the chest muscles, the biceps, and the front of the shoulders. Keep your back straight when doing it. Narrowing and lowering your contact points with the wall shifts the emphasis of the stretch from the shoulders to the chest. Rotating your elbows so that they face downward increases the biceps emphasis.

Photo 20 stretches the back of shoulders and many of the rotator muscles used to stabilize lock-offs. making this an important

stretch for climbers. Do it with your elbow high (chin level), low (breast level), and in between to stretch all the different divisions of the deltoid muscle.

Photo 21 stretches the rear deltoid, triceps, and latissimus muscles. Your "free" hand pulls the elbow of the stretching arm across and back behind your head.

For the exercise in photo 22, clasp your hands behind your back. To work up to this stretch, use a towel or a section of rope. If you alternate sides, this stretch combines the muscles targeted by the last stretch with those of the front side of the shoulder. Eighty-year-old Eiger pioneer Heinrich Harrer does this stretch daily by holding a piece of soap in both hands and washing his entire back.

Photo 23 stretches the forearms. Face your palms both up and down to stretch muscles on both sides of the forearms.

19

20

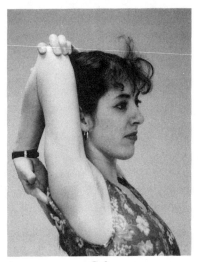

21

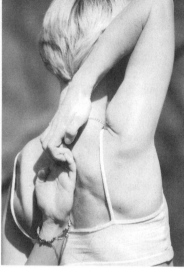

22

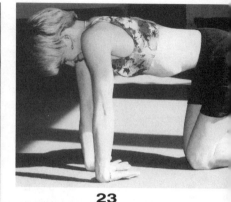

23

24

The preceding stretches covered the areas most important for climbing. If you need ideas for other stretch positions, consult books concentrating on flexibility.

USING GOOD FORM

Many athletes fail to maintain good postural integrity while stretching. The result for many climbers is lower back pain, knee problems, and other unnecessary pains.

In general, try to make your stretch positions focus tension on the muscles you're targeting and not on any joints. Doing your stretches with good form is much more valuable than reaching an extra inch in your stretch.

The following four examples illustrate the most common mistakes people make in stretching.

Front Splits

Turning the rear leg out to the side strains the inner ligaments of the knee (24). Athletes who regularly do this stretch incorrectly are prone to knee problems. For the same reason, avoid the so-called "hurdler's" stretch.

Photo 25 shows proper form: the front and rear legs are running parallel and the rear is knee facing straight down.

Toe Touch

If this common stretch is done with a round back, as in photo 26, it causes

25

lower back strain and nerve irritation. To keep this stretch healthy and helpful, always do it with your back totally straight (27).

Side Splits, Bent Forward

As with the toe touch stretch, keep your back straight in bending forward in the side splits. Your goal should be to touch

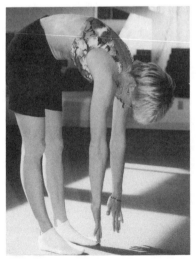

26

27

28

29

30

your belly (28), not your forehead (29), to the ground.

Abdominal Stretch

Photo 30 depicts a stretch especially useful after climbs that demand high body tension, such as caves and roofs. Make sure that your gluteal muscles are tightly contracted, as though you are pinching a penny between your buttocks. This distributes stress otherwise concentrated in the lower back.

CONCLUSIONS

We have outlined the best methods known for rapidly improving your flexibility. Remember that your body always tries to adapt to the ways that you use it. You will maximize your results if you bring your new ranges of movement opened by flexibility into your climbing and use them. In so doing, you weave flexibility into the other skills that help you move in the vertical world.

15. SCHEDULING AND PERIODIZATION

Equipped with the information from the preceding chapters, you now have the raw materials necessary for rapid improvement. Now we'll look at how to combine it all. In this chapter we will focus on how to organize your climbing and training during the days, weeks, months, and years that you climb.

SCHEDULING

Scheduling occurs at many levels. We can choose how long we rest between climbs and between climbing days. We can choose to have hard or easy weeks. We can plan for intense seasons and subdued periods. By understanding performance fluctuations, we can even organize successive phases of training to bring overall performance to a "peak" or a "valley" at a chosen time.

If you're mindful of the short- and long-term effects of training, scheduling can maximize your improvement. Good long-term scheduling insures that each stage of your training or climbing addresses the factors your body is ready for. Sound short-term scheduling minimizes the effects of accumulating fatigue on performance and training results. We'll begin by looking at short-term scheduling considerations that affect all climbers. Then we'll widen our focus to consider the more advanced scheduling concepts of periodization.

Resting between Climbs

The Strength Training chapter gave the recovery times for different types of physical exertion. Those times represented how long it takes a typical climber to repair the effects of training stress (muscle trauma, nervous fatigue, energy depletion, and so forth) in order to fully recover and reap strength gains (supercompensation) from the stimulus of a workout.

Although full recovery from training stress can take days, some factors, like the energy stores that fuel muscles, recover faster than others. Thus short-term cycles of fatigue and recovery occur due to the restoration of energy reserves during the minutes or hours that follow a hard effort. Although recovery of the muscle and nerve *structures* can take days, performance from one try to the next partly reflects the extent to which the *energy systems* that fuel performance recover between successive climbs or attempts. Since the ideal rest periods vary depending on which energy systems are depleted, let's examine optimal rest times for the different aspects of strength.

Power

When a climb uses power alone, a full recovery of the energy reserves it taps occurs within five to ten minutes of a maximum effort.

When doing a short, hard boulder problem or a difficult section of a route that demands only brief maximum strength, your power will continually decline due to muscular trauma and nervous fatigue. But rests longer than ten minutes add little to the recovery of energy stores that you can expect during the day. And since a full recovery of the non-energy-related factors takes two days, there's rarely reason to rest longer than ten minutes if what you're doing involves *only* power.

Power-endurance

Short-term recovery after power-endurance climbing depends on how quickly a climber can eliminate lactic acid from the crucial muscle groups. In general, it takes twenty to thirty minutes to remove half the lactic acid in your body. Fortunately, the high localized concentrations in climbers' arms dissipate more rapidly.

Strenuous power-endurance efforts warrant rests up to forty-five minutes or more. Longer rests can add a small margin of further recovery, but they typically mandate a second warm-up to reprepare a climber for strenuous activity.

Since feeling cold leads to a restriction of capillaries, it's important that the body be kept warm during such a long rest period. Moderate activity, like simply walking around, helps to keep blood moving throughout the body.

Local Endurance

If you have truly kept your muscles operating aerobically, a pure endurance workout should require almost no rest time to recover from. Although aerobic workouts do deplete muscle glycogen, they do it slowly enough that anyone with an adequate intake of calories can keep the pace of restoration in line with glycogen depletion for two or even three thirty-minute aerobic climbing sessions. Just remember that staying aerobic means not developing a pump.

Scheduling during a Climbing Day

If you climb enough hours during a day that accumulated fatigue will affect your climbing, scheduling can help you get the most from your reserves. If the climbs you plan to do involve several different types of strength, the order in which you do them affects how much of your potential you can access. And if you're interested in maximizing the training benefit of several different types of climbing, scheduling is a must.

Power First

Pure power climbing, like short, difficult boulder problems, is the most sensitive to fatigue accumulated from earlier climbs. Although the energy reserves that powerful climbing depletes are quickly restored, the *fatigue* it causes lowers maximum strength. Since power is very dependent on maximum strength (review the figure on page 97 in the Strength chapter), powerful routes and boulder problems are best climbed early in a climbing session before longer-duration climbs have fatigued the body.

Power-endurance Next

Power-endurance climbing relies less strongly on your maximum strength. So while maximum power could be jeopardized following a serious power-endurance effort, power-endurance is less compromised by a preceding power effort.

Endurance Last

Because endurance-oriented climbs demand only a low percentage of your maximum strength, they can be done without a major loss in ability after power and power-endurance efforts.

Remember that these are general guidelines to follow when other factors don't decide scheduling for you. If your day allows you time for one endurance-dependent route *and* time to check out some short, powerful bouldering, ask yourself which is more important to you. If you're equally motivated to perform on both types of terrain, following the above guidelines will maximize your overall performance. But if you're much more motivated for the endurance on-sight, you're best off doing it in your freshest state, even if it does compromise your power for the bouldering you feel ho-hum about.

Scheduling a Series of Climbing or Training Days

If planned correctly, successive climbing or training days can build ability faster than an alternating day on/day off schedule. But to keep from overburdening the body's recovery systems, care must be taken to ensure that successive days don't overfatigue particular systems.

Follow these guidelines to schedule days involving different strength emphases:

- Intense power days should be separated by two recovery days.
- Demanding power-endurance can be done one or two days in a row but should be followed by an equal number of recovery days.
- Depending on personal recovery, local endurance training can be done three to six days in a row, followed by only one or two recovery days.

To decide how to sequence consecutive climbing days between recovery days, apply the same principles we used to schedule efforts during a day. You don't have to do only power your first day, only power-endurance your second day, and only endurance your third day. But during three successive days of climbing, it's best to schedule your most powerful objective for the first day and save the more endurance-demanding efforts for the final day.

The table on the next page illustrates different sequences of climbing days and recovery days, showing sequences that provide both adequate and inadequate recovery. The schedules that provide adequate recovery can be repeated or combined, but realize that for most climbers they describe the *minimum requirement* for adequate recovery. Many climbers will require significantly more recovery time. Please pay attention to your personal recovery and use it as your ultimate guide.

PERIODIZATION OF TRAINING PHASES

Life is characterized by cycles, and human performance is no exception. Sometimes you just "have it"; other times you don't. Try as you might to create a steadily increasing level of performance, variations always creep in.

Letting these cycles occur unconsciously is undesirable, because our climbing must coordinate with seasons, work, vacation

Scheduling a Series of Climbing Days for Adequate Recovery								
Day 1	Day 2	Day 3	Day 4	Day 5	Day 6	Day 7	Day 8	Comments
Schedules that meet the minimum requirement of recovery time								
P	PE	E	R	R	Next Series			
P	PE	R	P	PE	R	R	Next Series	
PE	PE	R	R	E	E	E	R	Next Series
P	E	P	R	Next Series				
Schedules that provide insufficient recovery time								
PE	P	R	R	Power will be compromised on day 2.				
PE	PE	R	P	R	Insufficient recovery before day 4.			
E	PE	P	R	R	Sufficient recovery overall, but compromised performance due to poor sequence.			
Key: P = power-oriented day PE = power-endurance-oriented day E = endurance-oriented day R = recovery day				Acceptable substitutions: In any of the acceptable schedules, you may replace a P with a PE or E, or replace a PE with an E, and still have adequate recovery.				

time, and competition schedules. If we're having a "down" period, we usually can't postpone a climbing trip or a competition. And it's not uncommon for climbers to take a trip or enter a competition only to realize in retrospect that they climbed their best a month before or after it.

Periodization aims to solve these problems by organizing one's preparation so that peak periods can be reliably planned for and maximized. It is a technique for advanced athletes. Novice climbers, who typically have not developed the subskills that climbing relies upon, don't experience the performance fluctuations that periodization attempts to work with.

The Concepts of Periodization

In the 1950s, Russian scientist L. P. Matwejew scrutinized sports training. He wanted to know how athletes could maximize their athletic performance at a chosen time. In 1958 he laid out his periodization system based on a one-year repeating schedule. His ideas marked the birth of modern training science, and his underlying principles are still used in every major sport.

Periodization is founded on the following four ideas:

- The advantage of focus
- Cyclic variations in trained skills
- The importance of phase sequence
- Tying skills back together.

Focus

You improve fastest when you focus your training on one or two specific skill areas. This is partly because peripheral skills associated with any type of training must be mastered before real work can be undertaken.

Suppose, for example, you begin an intense bouldering phase to develop your power. If you haven't bouldered in a while, you spend the first few days worrying, learning about jumping off boulder problems, getting used to the pressure of high-intensity pulling on finger skin, and relearning the mental focus for short, maximum effort. Before real progress occurs, these background skills must become routine and take up only a small space in the back of your mind.

If you try to train several different skills at once, you spend too much time reacquainting yourself with the associated skills that each requires and not enough time actually pushing forward in any area. By contrast, focus puts the peripheral skills behind you, pushing you deeper into the real issues at hand. By focusing your energy on a simple, clearly defined objective, progress is virtually unstoppable.

Periodization thus breaks a training season into successive *phases* during which you focus on particular issues in your climbing. An individual training phase can last from a couple weeks to a few months.

Cyclic Variations in Trained Skills

Observing that homogeneous training doesn't always produce steady improvement, Matwejew asserted that trained ability in any well-developed skill has a certain ideal "life cycle." For example, although you may bring your power to its maximum one month, it's impossible to hold it steadily at its maximum level every month for a year.

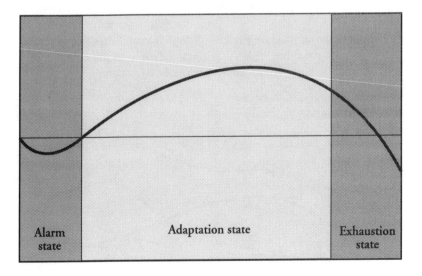

Alarm state

Adaptation state

Exhaustion state

The body's long-term response to training stress.

These cyclic fluctuations result from the competing effects of training adaptation and long-term fatigue.

In a body unadapted to a new workout, the stress of training may initially lower performance at the skill being trained. But the body soon enters an *adaptation state* in which appropriate levels of stress lead to supercompensation. In this state, training steadily improves performance in that area.

Serious long-term training in any one area leads to an accumulation of stresses and fatigue that eventually stall improvement if the body is not allowed a recovery period or a change in emphasis. Try hard for too many weeks or months at *anything* and you eventually reach a state of injury, illness, or burnout. Any prolonged stress eventually exhausts the faculties that recovery relies on. When this *exhaustion state* is reached, further improvement is impossible until that part of the body rests thoroughly.

By rotating through different phases, athletes improve while their bodies are receptive to it. Switching focuses before improvement tapers allows for continued improvement.

The cyclic quality of athletic performance fluctuations isn't always obvious. It can be obscured by the fact that overall performance represents the sum of many skills, each of which has its own particular cyclic variations. These individual variations occur simultaneously. Sometimes they complement each other; other times they cancel each other out.

Phase Sequence

Contrasts between the life cycles of different phases complicate the task of creating a peak performance phase. Some phases have short life cycles as a result of their stress on the body; ability in other skills fluctuates more gradually.

Conflicts between different phases further entangle the goal. Some training phases produce effects that are canceled out by the effects of others. We discussed in the Strength Training chapter, for example, how local endurance training can lower one's maximum recruitment.

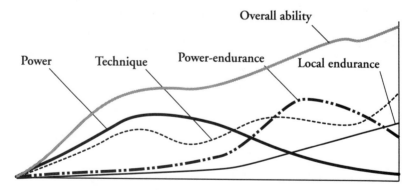

Overall ability represents the sum of subskill abilities.

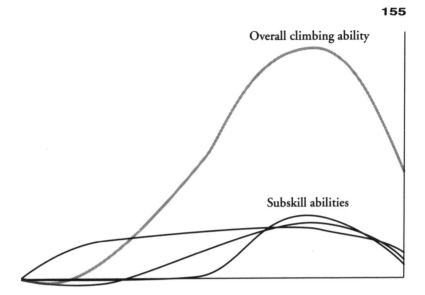

When different subskill abilities peak simultaneously, overall climbing ability soars.

As a result of these dissimilarities, different sequences of training phases can produce opposing results. Periodization thus requires a careful sequencing and timing of different periods of training focus to bring different subskills to their peaks simultaneously.

Tying It Back Together

Because success at on-sight and redpoint climbing requires refined ability in many areas, achieving peak performance requires dedicating at least one phase to tying the various skills together so that the climber has equal access to all the necessary skills. Although focus leads to the fastest improvement gains, it leaves athletes with relative weaknesses in the areas not emphasized. A final phase of *despecialization* helps climbers maximize their performance.

A periodized season therefore alternates specificity and diversity in training to give you focus during improvement phases and skill diversity during peak performance phases.

Building a Cycle from a Series of Phases

A training cycle is any sequence of training units that repeats itself. A macrocycle is the largest cycle that most athletes deal with. It consists of the training phases leading up to a peak phase and includes the recovery phase preceding the next macrocycle. A macrocycle can last from two to six months, so a year is broken into several consecutive macrocycles.

Each macrocycle is divided into four training phases that we'll examine in detail:

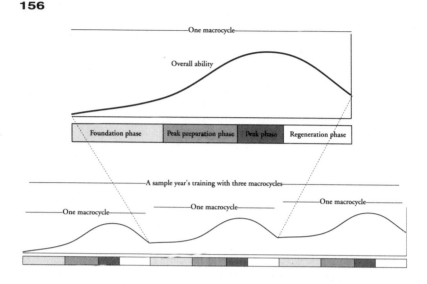

The phases of a macrocycle.

the foundation phase, the peak preparation phase, the peak phase, and the recovery phase. Effectively using a series of macrocycles and returning repeatedly to the same sequence of four phases resembles climbing a spiral staircase. As you wind your way around you keep returning to the same point in the cycle, but each time you find yourself at a higher level.

Following the guidelines we've described yields a periodized macrocycle. Max used one such macrocycle after reading our book (see the figure on the next page).

Max's first step in designing his periodized training plan involved clarifying his goals. He decided that he wanted to be in good shape for a mix of on-sight and red-point climbing when he reached his peak. The figure clarifies how Max's training time was distributed during his macrocycle and how his priorities changed during the phases

leading to a peak. A vertical slice through any point during the cycle reveals the time proportions spent on each particular focus. Midway through the foundation phase at time A, for example, Max spends approximately 45 percent of his strength training time on hypertrophy, 45 percent on local endurance, and just under 10 percent on general endurance. The technique bar shows that at time A he spends all his time on acquiring new techniques.

At time B, Max is more than halfway through his peak preparation period. He's been spending the biggest proportion of his time doing recruitment training in the form of short, powerful bouldering, but now he's starting to do more on-sight and redpoint climbing at his limit, easing into the power-endurance his peak phase will later emphasize. Once or twice a week he ends his bouldering sessions with a thirty-

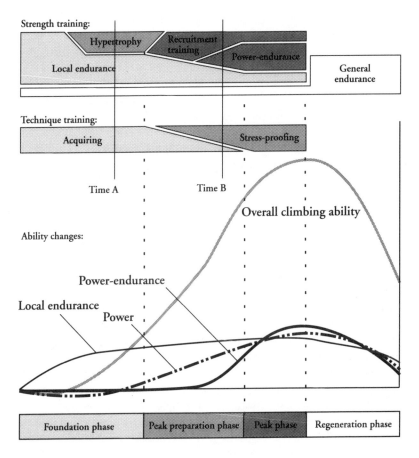

Max's periodized macrocycle.

minute easy climbing session for a local endurance workout. Of course, he still does a general endurance workout a couple times a week. He spends hardly any time acquiring techniques, concentrating instead on becoming proficient and comfortable with those he already has.

Below we'll look at the basic philosophy behind each phase, then explore what each involves in real terms for our test climber, Max.

Foundation Phase

The beginning phase of a new macrocycle aims to develop the base of climbing fitness that will be sharpened and honed in the next phase. It concentrates on aspects that take the longest to cultivate, or that would inhibit performance if they were emphasized just before peaking. The fitness base should prepare your body and make you more resistant to injury during the more intense phases to come. *The breadth of your foundation will determine the height of peak it can support.*

The heart of this phase is Max's local endurance training for aerobic energy restoration and capillarity (ARC). Max does one or two thirty- to forty-five-minute sessions of continuous climbing a day, four or five days a week.

The need for the early macrocycle phases to emphasize acquiring new technique engrams combines well with Max's local endurance training. The mandatory low intensity of thirty-minute ARC sessions on a climbing wall keeps the body in a fresh, receptive state for learning new technique. Max practices one or two particular techniques during each of his ARC sessions.

Though he's a long-time power junkie, Max must set aside his power cravings during this phase. If he does things right, his power may actually *decline* during this period. That makes this phase psychologically challenging for Max because (as the figure shows), though he works hard during this phase, his *overall* ability rises little, if at all.

Midway through the phase Max starts a hypertrophy program with weights twice a week. Scheduling it with plenty of time before his peak, Max still has time to hone his technique and raise his recruitment through more climbing-specific training later in the macrocycle.

Peak Preparation Phase

The peak preparation phase takes the foundation built in the preceding phase and fine-tunes it to the specific needs of climbing. It switches focuses to aspects that take a shorter time to develop, and to those that could have been sabotaged had they been placed earlier in the macrocycle. The peak preparation phase directs the momentum Max started in the foundation phase toward the climbing goals he hopes to achieve in the peak phase.

Training should be climbing-specific when possible, especially toward the end of this phase. The peak preparation phase carries the highest training intensity of the macrocycle, making attention to adequate recovery and early detection of possible injuries crucial.

For recruitment training, Max does short, hard boulder problems requiring maximum effort. He also works on a hard route he hopes to do at his peak, practicing the difficult single moves and linking short sections.

Midway through the phase, Max begins power-endurance training. He chooses routes that produce a burning pump, or he links together several boulder problems on his friend's climbing wall. He tries to make his power-endurance training closely simulate the type of climbing he hopes to do at his peak.

Throughout the phase, Max does an ever tapering amount of local endurance work. Because of the recovery-enhancing aspects of ARC training, he often finishes a climbing day with thirty minutes of continuous climbing on easy terrain.

For his technique, Max continues to acquire new techniques during his bouldering sessions, but he also begins to practice or "stress-proof" them by creating pressure situations with his friends and by using them in ever greater states of fatigue.

Peak Phase

Having done the preceding phases right, Max arrives at the peak phase with climbing's many subskills all peaking at once. With his individual peaks lined up, he climbs better than ever.

The individual peaks don't all have to be "off the charts" for Max's performance to be at record levels. The peak phase derives its power from the *collective, simultaneous* peaking of several of the abilities climbing involves. Because most styles of climbing rely on multiple skills, the impact of several moderately peaking abilities outweighs that of one or two record-level peaks.

Of course, planning a peak for a single, specific type of climbing (three-finger open-handed pocket strength on 113° limestone, for example) would require a more specifically targeted series of training phases.

The length of the peak period is roughly proportional to the duration of your preparation. The longer your foundation and peak preparation phases, the longer your peak will last. The gradual transition from foundation to peak phases represents a shift from quantity to quality as the climber moves from high-volume/low-intensity training toward lower-volume high-intensity workouts.

How Max climbs during his peak affects how long it lasts too. If he climbs constantly at his hardest, continually demanding the most from his ability to recover, he speeds the accumulation of fatigue and forces an abrupt slide in performance. With the intensity of the previous phase, Max can easily push himself into overtraining if he doesn't back off in intensity upon entering the

peak phase. If he draws from his abilities more moderately, he'll get more from his peak period. A thorough preparation has an incredible amount of "momentum," and an athlete's peak length has more to lose from continued training than from underuse.

Inevitably, when you arrive at a peak phase, you realize that some focus should have received greater emphasis, while others received too much attention. Simply note how your preparation could have been better and decide what changes you will make during your next macrocycle.

Don't make the mistake of spending your peak period trying to make up ground you failed to cover in the pre-peak phases. Although renewed focus might succeed in buoying one neglected ability, it would occur while all your other abilities fall gradually out of their peak. No peak period is perfect, and you're better off enjoying the richness of several honed abilities than bemoaning the lack of one or two abilities that came up short.

Recovery Phase

The final phase of Max's macrocycle gives him time off. This phase is *not* a setting aside of ambitions. A period of rest and recovery from extensive efforts is as crucial to further improvement as any of the preceding phases. And just as this phase allows closure and recovery from the periods of top performance, it can be equally regarded as an important *first* stage of the next macrocycle. Sufficient rest and distance from climbing prepares the body and mind to respond effectively to training anew.

The harder you have climbed and trained in the previous phases, the more important this time-out phase becomes. For full-time climbers, adequate recovery can take several weeks. This phase also allows them to capitalize on the important Reminiscence Effect discussed in chapter 3. If you're a recreational climber who has significant recovery periods built into your normal routine, this phase can be brief.

Macrocycle Summary

The illustration on page 157 shows how different phases are best arranged with respect to each other. It should be modified according to the skills one has already developed and one's natural propensities and disabilities. Someone who has developed strength through years in a weight gym should emphasize technique training as a priority over strength training. Someone with naturally poor recruitment would best enlarge his allotment of recruitment training at the expense of local endurance training. By contrast, one author of this book, a naturally high recruiter, can create performance peaks following extended macrocycles with only two to three weeks of recruitment training.

The observant reader will note that psychological training and flexibility were not mentioned in the text above. That's not because they have no place in periodized training. Instead, since psychological and flexibility training don't impose significant physical stress on the body, they don't suffer the cyclic fluctuations that other subskills do under intensive training. As a result, these are best pursued at an intensity appropriate to a climber's individual goals.

Challenges of Periodization

Periodization isn't for everyone. When you raise the performance peaks over those you normally experience, *you also deepen the valleys.* And to create a training phase, you must stay focused on particular types of training regardless of what "everyone else" is doing. Periodizing a macrocycle therefore presents psychological challenges to climbers who are used to more steady-state performance in their climbing.

Early in an endurance phase, for example, you'll often watch your power get worse before it gets better. It can be unmotivating to continue such training, especially if friends around you are reaching a power peak. But if you abort your endurance training and join in the training that brings them their rewards, you'll arrive at a state of high power without any endurance, and without any way to successfully bring both to a peak together.

Sticking to a periodization plan thus requires confidence in its results. Several points can help you maintain the conviction to keep on track with your own plan. First, know that top athletes in every sport periodize their training and endure the same fluctuations. Although when we see top athletes they're often performing at their best, they too take time off and have valley periods, when their performance is far below their own maximum potential and that of their peers.

A second aid to sticking to a plan is to involve a friend or coach in your periodization. A coach experienced with the outcomes of cyclic training brings an objective viewpoint unlikely to be swayed by the short-sighted perceptions that make many climbers want to abort a periodized plan early on. A coach can also make objective judgments about a climber's individual needs, priorities, and appropriate phase lengths.

Training with a partner who follows a similar periodized plan also reinforces dedication to the various phases of a macrocycle and can help prevent the temptation to end a recovery phase prematurely. Remember that training is a constant process of investments and payoffs. The bigger the investment, the greater the eventual payoff. So choose a plan you can stick to through its ups and downs. Don't forget that you have to enjoy the day-to-day *process* of your climbing and training to make big improvement. A training schedule that ignores your own satisfaction dooms you to frustration and diminished results.

Specializing Your Macrocycle

One consideration in tailoring your macrocycle to your needs is deciding on the type of climbing you want to bring to a peak. At climbing's cutting edge, redpoint and on-sight climbing could be regarded as two disciplines as dissimilar as the hundred-meter and ten-thousand-meter running events. No athlete can excel at both simultaneously.

You can perform up to your potential and make significant ongoing progress at redpointing and bouldering with only three days of climbing or training per week. To do the same at on-sight climbing requires a much greater volume of climbing, because it demands a vast repertoire of moves and a greater level of endurance.

Periodizing for a competition schedule requires juggling many diverse and sometimes conflicting factors, such as the negative influence of endurance training on power. Doing your best at one competition or a few events scheduled relatively close together requires building a peak and accepting the resulting valleys that bracket it. However, some extended competition series reward a climber who has consistent performances over the climber who beats him while peaking, but performs poorly during a subsequent valley. The specific timing and length of any periodized training plan must fit the objective.

As in all other sports, the cutting edge of climbing will evolve in the direction of ever greater specialization. Where today's top climbers can lead the sport in several avenues simultaneously, the same will not be true forever as good climbers learn how to train more specifically for carefully targeted goals. Güllich's 5.14c/d *Action Direct* and the disparity between Simon Nadin's competitive and redpoint performances signal the beginning of this trend.

The vast majority of climbers, however, will continue to draw their motivation from various sources. In doing so, they provide themselves with a wide platform from which to enjoy the many satisfactions climbing offers.

16. GENDER ISSUES

Climbing has long been a male-dominated sport. Credit this to social stereotypes, patrilineal power structures, or simple tradition. As rock climbing evolved from mountaineering, women faced larger social and economic obstacles to doing dangerous climbs in remote and harsh conditions. As a result, men have long outnumbered women at the cliffs.

Proportions, however, are changing fast. As climbing has become a sport of its own, many of its participants' orientations have shifted away from inherent danger to doing climbs for the satisfaction of personal challenge. With safety a prerequisite to regularly pushing one's personal limits, the climbing environment has become much more inviting to many would-be climbers. Add social changes to the sport's evolution, and the result is an influx of women to the sport on an unprecedented scale.

As in other sports, a leveling of abilities has accompanied the leveling of sexual proportions. Already female climbers have emerged whose performances place them among the top climbers of the world.

This chapter offers perspectives based on generalizations that hold true for a majority of women climbers. To avoid pitfalls to improvement, women must be aware of several consequences of the sport's sexual distributions and understand some physiological factors that differentiate them from climbing's majority.

DIFFERENCES

If only because of climbing's sexual proportions, many women have entered the sport via a man. Boyfriend, father, brother, or friend takes them out to introduce them to climbing, or more often, to show them *their* sport. This poses an insidious trap for women. For in walking into a lopsided sport, it's easy to make mistaken assumptions about the attitudes and qualities it demands of participants. In this male-dominated environment, it's easy to believe that the way men do it is the way it's done.

Big differences exist in the climbing style, training, and physical ideal that best suit climbers of different sexes. These differences are less the result of social and psychology conditioning than of simple morphology and biomechanics. The two sexes bring significantly different body-machines to the sport. Let's look at these differences and their effects on climbing.

Endurance Versus Power

On average, women have a greater percentage of slow-twitch muscle than do men. On rock, this translates to more endurance and less power. Having a comparatively greater reliance on endurance than strength, women more often benefit from taking the time to find the best sequence on an on-sight, even if it means hanging out on small holds for longer. Men, on the other hand, with greater reserves of power than endurance, more often find themselves in situations where it pays to choose a sequence quickly, even if it's not the easiest one, because it gets them to better holds quicker.

Flexibility

On average, women have and can acquire greater flexibility than men. This is a convenient accompaniment to their strength profile, since a wider range of motion offers a wider array of technique options on rock. Superior flexibility gives women more movement options, and superior endurance provides them the additional time to choose between them.

Size, Weight, and Height

Women in general are lighter in weight and have smaller joints than their male climbing counterparts. With respect to body and joint size, any given hold is thus bigger relative to a typical woman. Since women apply less force per area of hold, climbing is thus easier on their finger skin.

Combining these factors with height differences suggests that women's approaches to sequences will often be characteristically different from those of male climbers.

Power Centers

Female bodies are typically wider through the abdomen and hips than are those of males. This area is a woman's power center in climbing. The wider frame of attachment for the abdominal and gluteal muscles translates to a greater capacity for torsional stability and body tension from her power center.

Males have a larger skeletal structure in the ribs and shoulders. Their bodies more easily accommodate larger, stronger muscles in this area. With this as their dominant power center, maximum efforts in climbing will involve greater reliance on upper arm and shoulder strength. Their thinner waists are less effective levers for transferring torsional forces from the feet to the upper body.

These structural differences have predictable consequences at the crags. If you compare male and female climbers *of equal abilities,* you'll notice the women are nearly always stronger in the core and gluteal muscles and weaker in the upper arms and shoulders, and they have more endurance and less power.

Two climbers of equal abilities can have radically different strength profiles because they use their bodies in different ways. Consider making a move with a long static reach. The body must be positioned and stabilized so the free arm can reach to the next hold. For a man, the power center of the upper arms and shoulders best accomplishes this stabilization. These muscle groups brace the body, and the reach is made.

For women, effective use of their central core allows them to use *their* power center. With good foothold choice, the lower body can generate a twisting force that, relayed through the more powerful core, rolls the upper body on the shoulders in a twist-lock. With such an approach, many powerful reaches in climbing can be made with almost *no* bend at the elbows. When used effectively, a woman's stronger core easily compensates for her weaker shoulder area.

PERSONAL ASSESSMENT

This discussion underscores the importance for women of assessing their personal strengths and weaknesses relative to the female body. All areas of ability and strength can be developed. But since gains are easiest at your least-developed areas, it's important for every climber to understand the body she is dealing with.

Assessing herself by male standards, for example, a woman who has already trained her arm and shoulder power extensively can easily conclude that they still represent her weaknesses. In reality, they may be the most developed part of her physique. Meanwhile, although her core strength, endurance, flexibility, and even finger strength may be decent on a male scale, they may lag far behind in development relative to their potential.

The male profile of capacities is no perfect prescription for peak rock performance. In pursuing climbing fitness, women work toward a different ideal than men. The trap of pursuing men's ideals inevitably leaves many of their assets undeveloped and their potential unexplored.

CLIMBING TOGETHER

Unfortunately, with the differences between the sexes, it can be difficult for a woman to accurately access her strengths and weaknesses without spending time with other female climbers. Without external input from others with similar body-machines, it can be hard to know what your body is capable of.

Women thus have much to gain by climbing with other women. In the realm of technique, climbing together is especially helpful because it provides another mind to focus on solving sequence problems and offers vicarious feedback on techniques you may or may not have tried.

Of course it's important to practice and expose yourself to styles of climbing that don't come naturally to you. But because of climbing's sexual distributions, women get overexposed to the male style, and men are underexposed to how women—with different strengths—climb harder than they do. Thus, while many men could learn a lot from women who excel at the feminine style of climbing, few women need any more exposure than they already get to male climbing.

ROLE MODELS

Climbing technique is constantly evolving as people learn more effective ways of using their bodies. Today's top climbers use a significantly different climbing style than climbers did even five years ago. Any climber can gain by examining in detail the movement factors that help good climbers to climb well.

With the structural differences between the sexes, it's important that women have positive female role models for good technique. Gain what you can in both knowledge and inspiration from those who have dedicated vast time and energy to learning good body technique, by watching videos, attending competitions, or watching good climbers at the crag.

Because men and women do have biomechanical differences, some types of climbing better suit one sex than the other. But unlike gymnasts, climbers "compete" on the full spectrum of styles. The differences balance out. And at this point, there's a lot of mistaken stereotyping about what types of climbing women can excel at. Though the female side of the sport is underdeveloped at this point, our experiences have shown us that women can perform at an equal standard to men in climbing.

17. STAYING HEALTHY

"Face the simple fact before it
becomes involved.
Solve the small problem before
it becomes big.
The most involved fact in the world
Could have been faced when it was simple.
The biggest problem in the world
Could have been solved when it was small."
Lao Tzu, Tao Te Ching, verse 63[1]

This Chinese saying conveys an essential truth about climbing injuries. They rarely just happen like a bolt out of the blue. Most often they represent problems we failed to head off at an earlier stage.

AVOIDING INJURIES

Research has proven that most sports injuries—pulled muscles, tendinitis, strained ligaments—are caused by accumulated microtrauma (microscopic damage to muscle and connective tissue). The sudden onset of such an injury disguises the fact that it results from long-neglected mistakes in practice, in approach, or in care.

The good news is that you have to make repeated mistakes to get injured. The bad news is that these mistakes are easy to make, because the signs of accumulating microtrauma are rarely obvious.

Anytime you push your body to its limits, muscles and connective tissue suffer microscopic damage. With normal recovery, this damage heals before the next workout. The trauma is a normal part of the training process and prompts the body to make itself stronger. But when this microtrauma accumulates faster than the body can repair it, it sets the stage for what we normally think of as an injury: a sudden pain shooting up a muscle, or an audible *pop* from a ligament, signaling the tearing of tissue. Once sufficient microtrauma is present, even a movement you might normally execute without incident can cause injury.

Although the body is good at healing from injuries, it's not the same afterward. Nearly all body tissues heal with scar tissue, which is why the body rarely "forgets" an injury. Damage to muscle and connective tissues is thus well worth avoiding. Repeated injuries, even when optimally recovered from, can permanently reduce athletic potential.

The following tips will help you spot early warning signs of injuries and head them off before they come your way.

Adapt Gradually to New Stresses

Anytime you change the focus of your training or climbing, give yourself some extra time to adapt to the new stresses it might impose on your body. For example, being well adapted to crimping small holds after a summer of climbing at the City of Rocks doesn't mean you're ready to dive into the same grades of routes on your trip to Buoux,

[1] *Lao Tzu*, The Way of Life, *translated by Witter Bynner (New York: Capricorn Books, 1962),* 65–66 *(verse 63).*

where finger pockets are the rule. You can get some of this adaptation out of the way if you prepare for it in advance, but cutting transitions short risks injury.

Know When to Let Go

Working on Smith Rock's *Scarface,* Max stressed tendons in both forearms. The guilty move was a deadpoint for a two-finger pocket with the other hand at a one-finger pocket. When he pulled his tendons, his mistake wasn't doing the move imperfectly. This is the route's hardest move, and failing on it was understandable. His error was trying to hold the move as he fell backward, even though he got only one finger in the two-finger pocket at the top of his deadpoint.

If you're climbing on injury-promoting holds, or if you're injury prone due to past tissue damage, make a habit of letting go if you don't make a move in good form. Decelerating muscle pulls, where an athlete is lowering out of a position that he lacks the strength to hold, are 75 percent more common than accelerating muscle pulls. So on moves that could injure you, don't even *try* to hold on unless you do the move well.

Develop an Injury-avoiding Style

Too many climbers have an injury-prone climbing technique and philosophy. It's not a coincidence that climbers who always hang on at all costs, fight their way onward, catch every move by the skin of their teeth, and climb as if climbing is all strength are the ones most susceptible to injury. If any of these characteristics is a routine part of your climbing, beware. You're using a ram-

rod to open doors that are easily unlocked with proper technique.

The philosophy of pushing to and beyond your limits has its place in climbing—at a competition, for instance, or an important on-sight you've been waiting for. When this outlook is not a routine part of your climbing, you can safely afford to adopt it for such occasions. When it becomes the guiding philosophy of your day-to-day climbing, however, you're on the fast track to injury.

Be Willing to Change Plans

Be prepared to change your plans in your body's best interest. If you experience strains that feel like they verge on something worse, take a few days' break from the type of movement or positions that produce them. You might not get up a route as fast as you had hoped, but losing a day of climbing by being overcautious beats losing months because of injury.

Spread Out the Stress

People get injured at sites of excessive stress on their bodies. To reduce the chance of injury, spread out the stresses your body encounters.

If you crimp every hold you grab, you impose all the stress of hanging on to holds on the same limited number of sites in your fingers, hands, and arms. If you use a wider variety of grips, that same total quantity of stress is distributed among many more sites, each of which bears a smaller portion of the overall burden.

People whose style is excessively static overburden the elbow joints in lock-off positions; those whose style is excessively dynamic shift the emphasis to the shoulders and fingers. The point is that a balance of styles and activities offers the best way to resist injury, even when your training volume is high.

Forget Peer Pressure

Social scenes put big pressure on some people, and they may do things to impress the crowd or their peers that they wouldn't consider if they were alone. Notice when this happens to you, and take an extra five seconds to consider the possible consequences before you succumb to such pressure.

It takes a far-sighted self-discipline to say no to such temptations, but the payoff in injury-free climbing is well worth the effort.

Be Careful at the End Points of Movements

The end points or extremes in any joint's range of motion typically impose extra stress on the joints and muscles that surround them. A majority of injuries occur in these positions.

Keep this in mind when you assume such positions. At the bottom of a pullup, for example, when your arms are fully extended over your head, maintain muscle tension so your weight doesn't hang on your joints. When you relax muscle tension, the shoulder joints undergo dangerous stress. If you "drop" onto the joints either by relaxing the muscles or by getting too fatigued to support your weight muscularly, it stresses the ligaments surrounding the elbow and shoulder.

Avoid Painful Positions

Although they may be awkward, the positions you assume in your climbing shouldn't hurt you. When they do, something is wrong, and you may be risking injury. If a certain position routinely hurts you, figure out why. Work to correct the problem in a progressive, gradual way.

Consider Your Level of Development

Coaches in sports like gymnastics and figure skating, who plan athletes' careers years in advance, suggest that it takes four years for the body to adapt to handling major volumes of training and ten years for an athlete to reach his or her full potential. For a recreational athlete, these numbers could easily double. Keep in mind your personal level of athletic development in climbing when considering the amount of training impact your body can handle.

Train Antagonist Muscles

All joints in the body make trade-offs between mobility and stability. For extremely mobile joints like the shoulder, the balance of strength in the muscles that surround it provides stability. When some muscles gain disproportionate amounts of strength, it disrupts that balance, endangering the integrity of the entire joint.

If your climbing is well balanced, mixing slab climbing and overhangs, power routes and technical ones, climbing does not lead to dangerous muscle imbalances. If you emphasize specific training, however, muscle imbalances are possible, and you should take steps to avoid them. Anytime you put significant energy into acquiring new strength in one muscle group, take steps to strengthen the muscles that pull the limb or joint in the opposite direction. Spend at least one-half of the amount of time you dedicate to the target group on strengthening its antagonists.

For example, if you decide you want more pullup strength and begin a program of weighted pullups, balance the shoulder with some over-the-head presses, bench presses, and rotator cuff exercises.

Stretch the Muscles You Strengthen

When your body repairs the microtrauma caused by training, muscles heal slightly shorter. Thus when you selectively add strength to some muscles and not others, the progressive tightening of some muscles can reduce your range of motion.

Take the time to stretch the muscle you strengthen.

Heed Inflammation's Warning

Inflammation is the body's emergency response to any local injury, whether a burn, mosquito bite, or climbing injury. For infections and other injuries where there's a risk that damage might spread, it's a beneficial reaction. It enhances the blood supply and barricades the damaged area to limit the spread of foreign substances.

The swelling of a local climbing injury, however, has fewer benefits. Much of it comes from broken blood vessels whose leaking blood collects within a wound,

lengthening healing time. Inflamed tissues produce toxic substances that also slow healing. Since inflammation is an emergency response, ongoing inflammation that continues well after the initial trauma of a climbing injury indicates the failure of local healing mechanisms to cope with the injury's tissue repair needs.

When you experience inflammation, back off or stop altogether the activity that promotes it. To rehabilitate an injury, you *must* avoid exceeding the physical threshold that prompts further inflammation. If you do, the threshold between what you can handle and what causes further injury will continually rise.

Don't Suppress Symptoms with Medication

Many climbers reach for pain medications like ibuprofen whenever they feel pain in their joints or tendons. They rationalize it by saying that these drugs reduce inflammation, thereby promoting healing.

It's true that such medications reduce inflammation. They may indeed be appropriate whenever a fresh injury or reinjury prompts serious inflammation. But habitual use of these drugs is a mistake.

First, aspirin and ibuprofen block the body's production of prostaglandins, substances that play a vital role in the repair process. More important, pain relief medications mask symptoms that beg for your attention. Pain warns that problems will worsen if ignored; it exists to get you to change your behavior. When you climb on drugs, you shut down this important channel of communication. This leaves you wide open to do further damage to your injury or to experience new injuries.

When inflammation becomes chronic, as in chronic elbow or finger tendinitis, the activity that irritates the injury *must* be suspended. In such cases, anti-inflammatory medication can help to break a self-defeating cycle of overinflammation. Just don't try climbing or training when your injury is in such a condition. You should always aim to eliminate the need for such medications as quickly as possible.

If you need to take anti-inflammatory medication, you shouldn't be climbing. If you suffer repeated injuries, replace pills with skills and learn what it takes to avoid injuries.

Become Aware of Subtle Signs and Aggressively Avoid Them

Because of the role of accumulated micro-trauma in injuries, be aware of potential problems when they are still small, and act immediately to keep them from becoming big. If you look for subtle signs of trouble, you'll find there are plenty of cues that foreshadow injury. Most people simply disregard them through ignorance. They don't change their practices until warning signs escalate into injuries.

A seasoned athlete feels developing injuries *before* they occur and corrects the mistakes that made their inception possible.

RECOVERING FROM INJURIES

The extent to which an injury recovers depends partly on what you do during its recovery. Ignore an injury, or care for it haphazardly, and you may end up with a permanent loss of functioning. But learn about effective care and rehabilitation and apply it patiently, and you'll make the damaged part stronger and less injury prone than it was before its failure.

Here we'll offer general guidelines for what constitutes effective rehabilitation.

The first step when injury strikes is to evaluate its seriousness. Signs of potentially serious injury include:

- Severe or persistent muscle pain, swelling, or spasm
- Pain centered in a bone or joint
- Stiffness or restricted joint mobility
- Numbness or tingling.

If you experience any of these symptoms, stop exercising for five to seven days, then return carefully to training. Depending on the severity of your symptoms, consider seeing a doctor.

When to See a Doctor

Pain. All injuries cause pain. When the pain is severe, see a doctor.

Joint injuries. A doctor should examine most joint or ligament injuries. Immobilize the injured joint in the meantime.

Loss of mobility. If you can't move any body part normally because of pain or other reasons, see a doctor.

Persistent pain. If an injury doesn't respond positively to the steps below and show signs of improvement after two weeks, see a doctor.

It pays to err on the safe side. While being cautious might cost you more in the short term, it can save you months in recovery time. It also pays to seek out professionals who have experience with climbing injuries. Since climbing is not a mainstream sport, doctors experienced with its injuries are not common.

The Four Phases of Rehabilitation

Regardless of a doctor's role in your recovery, the responsibility for rehabilitation lies on your shoulders. An effective rehabilitation from an injury consists of four distinct phases.

Phase One: RICE

Remember the first-aid treatment for many sports injuries by the acronym RICE. It's appropriate for most acute sports injuries involving swelling. You're also wise to use RICE if you retraumatize an existing injury.

1. *Rest.* Stop using the injured part as soon as you hurt it. If you've done real damage, endorphins and other natural pain killers will probably reduce or even eliminate the pain within minutes, but don't let this tempt you to resume activity.
2. *Ice.* The leaking blood that collects within a wound lengthens healing time. Ice makes the blood vessels contract, limiting swelling. Cold

running water can be equally effective, and a creek might be the closest access to cooling for a climber's injuries.

3. *Compress.* Pressure also helps to limit the immediate swelling. Wrap the injured area with elastic wrap, tape, or cloth. Ideally the wrap should be snug but not tight. You don't want to shut off the blood supply.
4. *Elevate.* Raising the injured area above the level of the heart helps to drain excess fluid.

Phase Two: Range of Motion Exercises

Once you're past the acute phase of injury and inflammation is no longer a problem, phases two through four focus on rehabilitation. To understand their aims, we must first consider the role of blood in injury repair.

Blood is the main vehicle of healing. It carries white blood cells to fight infection and eliminate dead tissue, it brings nutrient building blocks and carries away waste products, and it ferries vital oxygen to the injury.

Typical healing times for different parts of the body are thus proportional to their blood supply. Skin and muscle tissue heal quickly because their dense capillary networks carry ample blood. Bones are also well supplied, which explains their remarkable ability to heal complete fractures. Because ligaments and tendons have few blood vessels, however, they can take six weeks or more to heal solidly. Cartilage has no blood supply. Surgery is the only solution to many cartilage injuries.

Although the number of blood vessels feeding a tissue affects its access to blood, *use* determines the circulation of blood within those vessels. Use promotes blood flow and stimulates injured parts to get stronger.

At early stages of rehabilitation, the injured tissue may be too fragile to tolerate significant movement. At this stage, aerobic exercise that doesn't directly involve the injured part helps increase circulation throughout the body and speed the healing process without using the injured area. Heat or gentle massage with ice also improves circulation.

Once an injury can accommodate direct use, tailoring the intensity with which you use an injured part to the stress it can accommodate without being further damaged improves circulation without traumatizing the tissue.

Before beginning phase two, decide whether you're *ready* to use your injured area. If you experience any of the following symptoms, hold off before moving to phases two through four.

- If you get sharp pain on use
- If pain gets worse during your training
- If pain is worse the morning after using it.

Appropriate use of an injury may produce some discomfort or aching in your injury, but *stop* if you experience sharp pain.

The first stage of use involves simply moving the injured joint or limb through its comfortable range of motion. It should involve no resistance at all. This serves to relax the normal tightening that occurs when damaged tissue repairs, and it helps restore normal mobility to the limb or joint.

Move the injured joint or limb through as much of its normal range of motion as you can without experiencing pain. At first this range may be severely reduced from its normal healthy range. Over time, however, it approaches its normal extent.

Sometimes a limited range of motion (which can result from strengthening the muscles without stretching them) contributes to the development of an injury. Although it's too early to start an aggressive stretching program for the injured area, consider whether a limited range of motion played a role in your injury.

Phase Three: Progressive Resistance Exercises

Once the injured area can move under its own power through its full range of motion without pain, apply resistance to strengthen the damaged tissues. Figure out the exact motions that call the injured tissues into play, and perform these motions against a resistance. At first the slightest resistance may be a sufficient stimulus. Progress at the pace your body dictates. Let pain warn you of overdoing it.

The following anecdote illustrates tailoring the intensity of use to what the injury can handle without further damage. During one of Jerry Moffat's first trips to the United States, he saw John Bachar intently raising his hand up and down as if pretending to lift a weight, while his other hand stabilized his elbow. "What are you doing?" Moffat asked. "Curls," responded Bachar. He was suffering from a serious elbow tendon injury, and the mere weight of his own arm provided an appropriate level of resistance for Bachar's condition. He went on to recover from his elbow tendinitis and climb at a high standard.

During periods of inactivity, heat can help increase blood supply and relax muscles. Just don't use heat on an injured muscle within twelve hours of resistance exercises.

This phase is also a good time to consider whether muscle imbalances played a role in your injury. If the injury lies in a muscle or tendon, look for overly strong or weak antagonists to the injured tissue. For a joint injury, look for strength imbalances in the muscles that act across the joint. Take this opportunity to strengthen any weak (uninjured) muscles that may have contributed to your injury.

Phase Four: Reintegrating the Injured Part

Once you can use the injured tissue against resistance without pain and it has recovered at least two-thirds of its normal strength, it's time to begin using it in climbing-specific ways. For an injured muscle, this serves to reintegrate it with its muscular partners. Climbing movements involve the cooperative efforts of groups of muscles, and when an injured muscle or muscle tendon unit has gone unused for some time, it must be "reeducated" before it can work in concert with the other muscles involved in climbing movements.

For a joint injury, this phase gradually reintroduces it to the specific stresses demanded of it in climbing. Begin with easy climbing movements, and try using the injured part at a low intensity on all the positions, movements, and speeds that you might encounter in normal climbing. Expose the injured part to a wide diversity of movements, and increase the difficulty gradually over a period of several days or weeks to restore full use. Even if the injury is 90 percent healed before this phase, ignoring this process can thwart full recovery.

Phase four is a good time to consider how technique might have contributed to your injury. Do you climb with an excessively dynamic (or static) style? Do you "drop" onto your joints? Do you always crimp? Do you climb only overhanging routes? If you answer yes to any of these questions, diversify your approach to climbing to spread its stresses more evenly throughout your body, and reduce the likelihood of injury.

One of the challenges of rehabilitation is deciding when you're ready to move from one phase to the next. The following table provides a guideline for the duration of the phases we've discussed. But make your body the final judge.

How Long Should Each Phase Take?		
	Muscle injury	Connective tissue injury (tendons, ligaments, or cartilage)
Phase 1	1–3 days	3 days–2 weeks
Phase 2	1–3 days	3 days–6 weeks
Phase 3	1–3 days	1–6 weeks
Phase 4	1–2 weeks	1–6 weeks

PERSPECTIVES ON INJURY

Don't make the mistake of regarding injuries as simple misfortune. Of course it's unfortunate to suffer the setback they induce. But often it is only through such setbacks that climbers become aware of the need to change negative practices. Injuries are your body's last attempt to tell you something when subtler messages go ignored. If you'll take the time to understand your injuries, you'll grow as an athlete.

Most top athletes have a story to tell of how injury made way for a new chapter in their athletic development. Often a particular injury forced them to refine their instinctive awareness and develop a keen intuitive perception of the fine line between appropriate and excessive training. Injuries can help climbers understand the basic importance of knowing and accepting their personal athletic nature.

It's not fair that some climbers can climb twice as hard, rest half as long, and still have no problems with recovery or injury. But your body responds according to what is true for you personally, not to what is "fair." The faster you accept this and learn what *is* true for you in terms of your athletic constitution and recovery, the healthier you'll be and the better you'll climb.

Don't think that the best climbers are always the ones with the greatest injury resistance or the quickest athletic recovery. The best climbers are those who accept and work within their personal constraints, whatever they may be.

Injuries don't have to mark an over-the-hill point in your climbing career. Over and over, climbers who identify the causes of their injuries, and have the patience and dedication to continually reinvent their approach to climbing, go on to surpass themselves and reach new peaks in performance.

OVERTRAINING

How much is too much? More training is certainly not always better, because the body has a finite ability to recover from the stresses of training.

We each have a threshold representing the maximum training volume we can healthily adapt to. Exceed the threshold and you're overtraining, adding stress to your body faster than it can recover. If you keep it up, improvement stalls and injuries follow. Ambitious athletes risk overtraining because improvement comes fastest when they approach this threshold without exceeding it. They constantly try to go as close to it as they dare without stepping over the line.

Unfortunately, this threshold constantly changes. As you improve and become capable of harder workouts and routes formerly impossible for you, the threshold rises. If you take a season off, it descends and you must restart at an easier level than where you left off. When you have a surplus of stress in your life, it will be lower than at times when your life feels more relaxed. Finally, everyone's threshold lies at a different level. Like it or not, some people are simply born with a greater ability to recover from physical stress than others.

If you knew where you stood with respect to your personal overtraining threshold, knowing how much or how hard to train would be easy. Unfortunately, it's rarely obvious. Since the stress of overtraining is often distributed over several systems and muscle groups, overtraining doesn't lead immediately to acute injuries, but rather to a growing accumulation of stress and microtrauma throughout the body. Before obvious symptoms occur, an athlete may overtrain for weeks during which the potential for injury gradually grows and improvement falters.

Fortunately, many signs warn of overtraining. Too many climbers simply make a habit of ignoring them.

Healthy training requires striking a balance between stress and recovery. Since big problems start out small, pay attention to subtle signs.

Signs of Overtraining

Joint stiffness with loss of motion
Localized pain, usually in a joint
Soreness that won't go away
Inability to have really good days
Stiffness, swelling, and pain on waking up
No athletic improvement, even with rest
Bad or reduced coordination, even when fresh
Change of bone, muscle, or joint contour
Burning sensation, tingling, or numbness in limb
Regression despite continued or increased training
Problems sleeping

PLATEAUS

Athletes in all sports experience periods of nonimprovement when, try as they might, they can't break through to higher levels of ability. Scientifically, plateaus are a challenge: top athletes in all sports report experiencing them, yet science can't pinpoint a cause. As a result, no singular prescription for ending them exists.

Why all the confusion? Plateaus can result from any of several unrelated causes.

We've described solutions to these problems throughout the different chapters of this book. The key is to figure out which of these factors is behind *your* plateau and act to address its specific needs. Even if you can't identify your particular problem, let plateaus prompt you to *change* some aspect of your climbing or training. Your body, mind, and soul need fresh stimuli to progress.

Some Causes of Plateaus

Overtraining
Goals too high or too low
Boredom with a particular climbing area
Working only on your strong points; neglecting weak areas
An approach that ignores the principles of effective training
Sticking with one type of training too long
An excess of one kind of climbing
Insufficient fitness base

18. TACTICS

Tactics are intentional strategies and intellectual steps that maximize success on routes. Unlike psychological approaches, which involve attempts to adjust one's level of arousal, tactics begin as conscious, rational thought processes that aim toward more specific goals. We'll discuss tactics for maximizing success at several different aspects of climbing.

REDPOINT TACTICS

We all have physical limitations concerning the ultimate level of difficulty we can climb. But whether your current limit lies at 5.7 or 5.15, how nearly you approach your personal limit on a route depends on how well you use the abilities you have.

While working on a redpoint over the course of a few days, people make negligible strength gains. They redpoint much harder routes than they can on-sight because rehearsal allows them to eliminate and correct *errors* in their sequences, technique, pacing, and hold choice. By eliminating these errors with practice on a route, a climber can approach the maximum potential that his or her combined abilities make possible at that stage of development.

The allure of a hard redpoint, regardless of one's ability, is the near perfection required to climb up to your potential. The experience of climbing with that perfection during the final ascent is not quickly forgotten.

Since rehearsing a route provides the chance to reflect and consider your approach between tries or days, tactics dramatically affect redpoint ability. To a large extent, tactics determine which routes fall within your reach and which lie beyond.

Choosing a Route to Work On

Many climbers who are insecure about their redpoint ability choose to work on routes that are much too hard for them. The solace of such a choice is that it relieves the expectation of actually doing the route, removing the anxiety that accompanies the potential for success. But since the satisfaction of accomplishment is reserved for those routes you actually do, the question is which routes *will* you do, given your time and ability.

Long, drawn-out efforts on overly difficult routes run counter to the essential idea of redpointing, and they stall the process of improving. Redpointing is about eliminating errors to allow your maximum potential to apply itself to the climb in question. After more than eight or ten days working on a route, climbers rarely continue to uncover errors. Instead, they hope to make gains in ability while working on the route. In such cases, a climber's overall ability would improve faster by other means, and he's better off leaving the project and returning when he's a fitter climber.

If you're new to the redpointing game, choose a route just one letter grade above your hardest on-sight. Increase the margin between your on-sight and redpoint efforts only when you've experienced redpoint success on climbs of that range.

Eliminating Errors in Single Moves

Once you've chosen your route, it's time to get to work. The first order of business is to learn how to do the route's hardest individual moves.

Your ability to do any given move results from your knowledge about the move and the physical resources you have available when you try it. The first time you try a move, you have very limited information about it. You know only how the holds appear from below and how you've handled similar-looking situations in the past. When you make a move with such limited information, you tend to use unnecessary energy to accomplish it. With practice, however, you learn which aspects of your efforts are useful and which are extraneous or counterproductive. You learn to eliminate unnecessary movements and relax all but the muscles the move demands. As you get a move more and more "wired," the amount of energy you expend on it decreases.

Learning the hard moves on a route you hope to redpoint involves learning new *move-specific techniques*. Since you learn technique best when fresh, begin work on a route by assessing where its hardest moves lie and zeroing in on them. Rest on the rope frequently at this point to avoid the accumulation of fatigue and the technical ineptitude that results. Link together only the minimum number of moves necessary to decipher the best sequence.

Linking Moves Together

Once you know how to do the single moves, you must learn how they link together. If you have trouble figuring out a sequence that works, or choosing between two sequences that seem equally suitable, try down-sequencing that section: look above the section that stumps you and decide which hands you'll want on the holds that lie there. Then figure out which hold choices preceding that section will allow you to get there in sequence. Continue this process downward until you reach the tricky section. The final sequence you arrive at thus represents not only the result of the sequences that preceded it but also an awareness of the sequences that follow. By considering what came before and what comes after each section, you can arrive at the optimal sequence.

Spreading the Fatigue

Hard redpoints often challenge us because of the accumulation of muscle-specific fatigue. For example, if a long, vertical, crimpy wall were followed by a steeper thirty-foot section of the same difficulty involving long reaches off bigger holds, you'd probably have no problem finishing the route. Your fatigued crimp muscles would get a break on the final headwall, and your lock-off muscles would get a relative rest on the first part of the route. But when the same long, crimpy wall is followed by another thirty feet of the same kind of climbing, the buildup of fatigue in specific muscles (in this case your crimp-specific muscles) could be your downfall. Learning to spread accumulating fatigue to other parts of your body can help to diffuse the problem and maximize your ability to use the strength resources you have.

In redpoint climbing, you have the advantage of being able to plan for the route as a whole before attempting a final complete ascent. As a result, you can consciously alter your style and approach on early sections of a route in ways that best conserve the resources that upper sections demand. This can lead you into some initially counterintuitive measures. Using a handhold in the style that feels the best and easiest is not always tactical on a worked route. Sometimes a hand position or grip that feels second-best is more strategic for linking moves because it allows you to save a specific kind of strength needed higher on the route.

For example, if the upper section of a route involves difficult crimping, you can make a conscious effort to use open grips on the lower portions of the route. Open grips may not be the optimal way to grip the holds on the lower section, but if they can conserve your much-needed crimp strength for the upper cruxes, it's worth it.

Other tactics to spread the fatigue include the following:

- Trading off between different sets of fingers in finger pockets
- Loading your thumb on edges to relieve weight from your fingers
- Using the outer edge of your palm to grip buckets and give your fingers a rest
- Dynoing easier moves low on a route to preserve your static locking power for a lock-off crux higher up
- Tiring your legs in a strenuous stem rest to recover your arm strength
- Tiring your arms by hanging on handholds to recover leg and foot strength.

Simply doing what comes naturally cannot be relied upon for efficient redpointing. The instinctive method often best suits the moves you're on, but when redpointing, your approach to any particular move must be made in view of all the moves that lie ahead. You have to consider the whole package and think *strategically* about what will make the whole route best fit together.

Planning Your Clips and Chalk Stops

If you take the trouble to figure out a viable sequence on a route you're working on, take the time to incorporate the positions in which you'll clip in and chalk up.

In choosing these strategic holds, don't make the mistake of trying to clip in too early. Clipping at arm's length above you can require six feet of extra slack. This not only yields a longer fall in the event of slipping off just before clipping, it also takes longer to get the rope up and into the carabiner, especially if your belayer gives out rope slowly. Clip from the best holds you can, even if it means climbing a few moves higher before stopping for the clip. The best hold is not always the position that feels easiest while working the route. Instead, choose the position that least fatigues the important muscles demanded higher on your route.

Planning for the Intimidation of Leading

If you work a route on top-rope, you must also account for the fact that climbing it may be more intimidating on lead. If you know that lead intimidation will be a factor, do some of your preparatory linkages on lead. Lower to a bolt or piece of protection at the point where your linkage begins. After making sure you can safely do so, clip in, untie, pull the rope, and retie for the next link.

Eliminating Errors in Sequences of Moves

After you've worked out how to do the individual moves on a route, you're ready to start linking successive moves together. On a hard route, a successful redpoint at this juncture is unlikely, but you might as well start trying the route from the ground and seeing how high you can get without falling, right?

Wrong! Linking sections of the route from the ground teaches you little of what you really need to know to redpoint a route. Don't waste the time and energy on

A failed redpoint attempt on The Monkey Face.

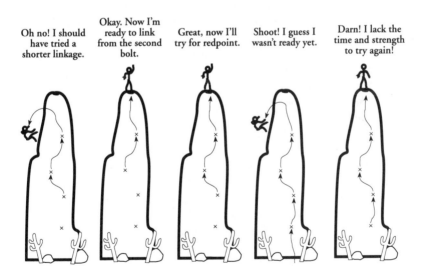

Overambitious choices of linkages make working a route a slow, frustrating process

an attempt that doesn't get you a step closer to a successful redpoint.

Why are linkages from the ground tactically inefficient? Since we're trying to figure out how to do the route as quickly as possible, approach this question by considering the minimum learning needs for a redpoint. After all, there's no point in learning superfluous information—the more time you spend learning unnecessary things about a route, the longer you'll take before redpointing it.

Imagine a route where every move is roughly the same difficulty. If the route is at your limit, you'll start out fresh and get progressively more tired as you ascend. Since fatigue reduces one's ability to use good technique (see chapter 3), you'll need to have practiced the higher moves much more than the lower moves just to be able to climb them with comparable technique. In fact, other factors being equal, the higher a particular move lies on a route, the more practice it will require for you to be able to successfully do it on redpoint.

Therefore, the key question to ask when considering how to plan the next session on the rope is not "How high could I redpoint on my next go from the ground?" It's "What's the biggest linkage I could do to the *top* of the route?" Early on you may only be able to link the final third of a route. With practice, however, you'll be able to start your successful practice linkages at lower and lower spots.

When successive attempts consist of progressively longer links to the route's finish, you climb the first moves the least, the middle moves somewhat more, and the top moves the most. As a psychological bonus, by topping out each time you're practicing *success* on the route, ingraining the feeling of reaching the anchors over and over.

The key to this process is to accurately predict your link ability as it gradually improves and to choose successive link-up goals in an incremental fashion. Plan your intended linkage carefully, based on previous linkages you've done on the route. And when forecasting what you'll be able to do on your next linkage, guess conservatively: falling off as a result of an overambitious link can waste a lot of time and energy. Imagine, for example, that while working on a route, you suspect you're capable of linking from between the second and third bolts of a route to the top. If you ambitiously decide to start from the second but fail, you'll probably want to start from the third bolt in order to have success on your next attempt. By overestimating what you can link, you slow the process of learning to redpoint a route by temporarily reversing your forward progression of ever longer linkages.

If instead you choose your linkage conservatively, you'll link a longer section of the route each try. If in the above example you had chosen to start your first linkage from the third bolt, you'd be ready for a successful link from the second or below on your next try. Although conservative linkages move you toward your redpoint goal in smaller steps, they often get you there faster.

Ideally, your growing knowledge of the moves and techniques the climb demands increases one step ahead of your growing

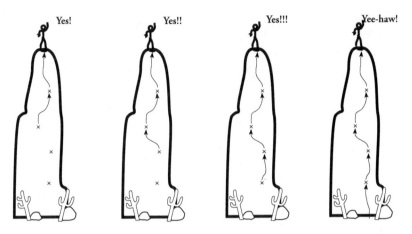

Yes!   Yes!!   Yes!!!   Yee-haw!

Conservative choices of practice links lead to the quickest redpoints.

fatigue during successive efforts. That way, successive efforts naturally stress-proof your technique on those specific moves as you practice them in progressively greater states of fatigue.

Of course, this strategy must be adapted to the particular route you're on. If there's a low crux on the route, you'll probably have to work it more than the top of the pitch. The point is that the amount of learning required for any particular move depends on *where* that move lies within the route as a whole. Climbers who regularly succeed at 5.12 have been shut down by 5.8 moves when they come after strenuous, strength- and technique-draining sequences.

Mental Training

Since working on a route allows you to mentally review it between attempts or between days on the route, mental training can maximize the benefits of your practice.

(Review chapter 4, Technique Training: Practice, for more on mental training.)

To use mental training to help practice and solidify your sequence of moves, close your eyes and do your climb in your mind, paying close attention to the exact sequence of moves and holds that you use in reality. Some people like to give different moves key words to help remember them ("twist," "reach," "dyno," "hop"). If there's a section you can't remember, make that section a priority on your next climbing attempt.

As you do the sequence in your mind, make sure that there are no points of hesitation. If there is one in your visualization it will likely appear in your climbing. Find out why you hesitate at that point, and practice that section of the route until the hesitation is gone.

Once you know the complete sequence, you can mentally practice it in different ways to help ingrain it. For example, do your route mentally at high speed and then

Mental training can help you solidify your sequence of moves.

in slow motion. Climb it both from within your body, seeing the route as you normally would, and as a spectator, watching yourself execute the moves you know. When you can do all these mental rehearsals without hesitation, chances are you'll have the sequence flawlessly ingrained in your mind.

When you know your route to this extent, your movements begin to flow together. Your fingers assume the shape of the next hold before reaching it. Once they're on it, the next foot move is already in progress, and the climb is no longer a succession of individual moves but a single unbroken orchestration of perfected movement.

ON-SIGHT CLIMBING TACTICS

Achieving success at redpoints relies heavily on planning and replanning the route from the comfort of a rest position. On-sight climbing offers a one-shot chance at success, making it a completely different game. As a result, *attention* is the critical resource when considering tactical approaches to on-sight climbing. How the climber uses her attention during the limited time at her disposal will determine how much she can get from her strength and technique during an on-sight.

It takes an incredible flexibility of attention to juggle the different demands a challenging on-sight imposes. A climber must be able to focus her fullest intensity of awareness on the kinesthetic demands of a single move, without losing sight during the less intense moments on a route of how the pitch as a whole fits together.

As a result, a proficient on-sight climber learns how and when to change the *focus* of her attention. When the moves she is making don't demand 100 percent of her attention, the climber zooms out to consider upcoming moves and continually reviews her overall approach to the route. On sections that demand total focus and ability, her attention zooms in to exclude all but the immediate moves being made.

Zooming Out

On-sight tactics begin before a climber leaves the ground. From a route's base, she can size up its basic character and get partial answers to questions like:

- How long is the route?
- Are there rests that divide the route into sections?
- What would be an appropriate pacing during these sections?
- Where will the protection be clipped?
- Are there dangerous sections of the route?
- Are there any obvious sequences the route will demand?

On-sight climbers instinctively spread out their fatigue among muscle groups (see Redpoint Tactics) when they're pumped. For example, a climber will try alternative grip styles once she's too pumped to crimp a flat edge. But by that time, lactic

From a zoomed-out perspective, a climber considers the climbing ahead.

acid levels in the muscles have usually pushed the climber beyond the point of recovering on the route.

Approaching an on-sight climb tactically requires *anticipating* the fatigue it will impose before it strikes. When you're zoomed out from the moves you're on, keep an eye on the climbing ahead of you. If the moves ahead will demand difficult crimping, try open-handed positions, or use your thumb when you can to rest your other fingers. If a route involves sustained finger pockets, start varying the fingers you use *before* your best pocket-pulling fingers fatigue.

Zooming In

A climber can rarely complete a challenging on-sight climb from a continually zoomed-out perspective. Being able to recruit the most muscle fibers possible and make the best use of your technique requires your full attention. As a result, succeeding at the crux sections of challenging on-sights demands the ability to zoom in on the moves you're making and set aside other concerns. At the critical moments when an on-sight pushes you to your limit, your awareness must condense to a single point in time, containing nothing but an evolving present moment.

Most climbers find it difficult to achieve this level of focus because it requires taking awareness away from other factors that beg for your attention. When you're 100-percent focused you forget the rope, the protection, the fall, and the moves that will follow those you're on. Forgetting these other factors for even a moment can cause panic the first few times it happens. But much of the urgency of these moments is perceptual.

After just a little experience climbing, we learn that it's okay to be pumped on a route. It doesn't mean that you're about to fall off. Yet to a beginner on lead, that same level of pump sends panic signals all over her body. The difference is perceptual. Making the perceptual shift from the beginner's reaction to the expert's calm overview requires accepting some of the terrifically uncomfortable feelings that climbing on-sight at your limit can give you.

Although it never hurts to strive for control in climbing, succeeding at the cruxes of challenging on-sights requires an acceptance of its absence. The feeling of control vanishes when you flirt with the limits of your ability. The best climbers may look like they're always in control, but they feel the same urgency as most people do when they climb at their limit. The difference lies in their *response* to that urgency.

Success and failure hinge on how you react during the brief moments when everything verges on failure. In many cases, you've already climbed through the most difficult moves before reaching this state. With just a few more feet, better holds await and you'll be able to recover. But for the moment, your forearms are exploding, your hands are opening, and the lactic acid level in your blood has decreased your coordination drastically. No matter what your level, these uncomfortable instants are the essence of on-sight climbing at your limit.

One way to stay zoomed in is to borrow a mind-set brought to climbing by competition events. In such events, competitors are ranked whether they complete the route or not based on the high point they reach. As a result, even climbers who are unlikely to reach the top try their hardest until they fall off, because climbing just one or two more feet can improve their final rank. When their muscles verge on failure and they feel they're about to fall, the desire to climb just two more feet keeps their focus on the moves immediately before them.

By keeping them pushing farther, even when their chances for finishing the route look bleak, this philosophy sometimes gets them through to rests from which they can recover and complete the route. The extra attention they recruit by setting aside their overall objective and bringing their entire focus to the move they're making gets them through cruxes they would otherwise fall off.

This approach helps climbers disregard the pessimistic outlooks that accompany the feeling of a pump. If the route you're attempting is of a grade that's within your on-sight potential, impossibility is only an illusion pulled over your eyes to provide you an excuse to give up when it hurts.

Ideally, a climber's attention continues to narrow as she nears the route's finish, because the on-sight climber's perspective looks only forward to what awaits, not backward. When only a few moves remain, even a zoomed-out perspective needs to contain only the final moves, so a successful on-sight finishes in a crescendo of pure focused attention.

Training for On-sight Climbing

On-sight climbing requires being comfortable with uncertainty while making and acting quickly on intuitive judgments. As a result, on-sight skill benefits from great volumes of on-sight climbing.

Although doing laps on a training route can efficiently boost your strength, it can actually harm your on-sight ability, because you develop the habit of knowing what moves to make next. Lap climbing develops a habit of climbing in control, on mental autopilot. Developing comfort in doing moves at your limit requires the opposite: a climber must learn to maintain mental "poise" even when she is barely hanging on to holds.

One way to promote comfort with the unfamiliarity of on-sight climbing is to get as much experience as possible on different types of rock. First, your on-sight climbing ability benefits as you learn how a particular rock type lends itself to climbing. But more important, experiencing *variety* in your training and climbing adapts you to reading the rock and using whatever techniques it asks for. Climbers who climb in only one area inevitably develop the habit of using the narrow range of techniques their area demands.

Speed climbing helps climbers get accustomed to making quick decisions and acting on them. Choose on-sight climbs well below your limit that you know to be safe. For the best results, compare your time on the route to that of your partner. The point of timing your climbs is not to establish who is faster, but rather to provide a stronger impetus to climb quickly. In a climbing gym setting, stick training with a partner (see chapter 4) can provide a fresh way to continually do "new" moves through bouldering.

The best on-sight climbers don't think about the factors we've discussed when they're on routes, although they climb according to such principles. These and other tactics like them guide their movements unconsciously.

Following the advice of this section will fill your mind with so many rational thought processes that your on-sight ability may temporarily decline. But that's not a condemnation of our suggestions. It implies that before these tactics will benefit your on-sight ability, you must have enough experience with them for them to operate silently, without conscious contemplation. The best way to bring them to this stage is to practice putting them to use on large quantities of on-sight climbs at a difficulty well below your on-sight limit.

THE PROGRESSION PYRAMID

In day-to-day climbing, uncertainty often surrounds the issue of quantity versus quality. That is, do you benefit most from spending time on a few routes at your limit, or from doing more routes well within your ability? This uncertainty can often be most evident just after you've reached a new high in the form of your hardest redpoint or hardest flash. "Does this mean that this is my new level and I should just work on routes of this grade now?"

For example, Max made a big leap forward during a spring trip to France in 1987. After a winter of committed strength, finger, and flexibility training, he pushed his top redpoint grade from 13b to 13d in one climbing season. After these successes in midseason, Max decided that this must be his new level and that he should concentrate only on routes of that grade. "Why not add a few more 13c's and d's while I'm on a roll?" he figured.

Yet this new policy led not to more successes but to frustration, sickness, and ultimately injuries necessitating months of recovery. His approach at the crag took Max from exhilarating progress to convalescence in two short months.

Looking back at the previous year, Max realized that his progress, which had seemed to start with his gratifying efforts in France, actually had its beginnings seven months before leaving home. Although his previous season at home had not been his first of climbing 5.13a, it had consisted of forming a wide base of diverse routes in the 12d to 13a range. Looking back, Max concluded it was this broadening of his platform of experience and strength in the underlying grades that had allowed him to make a spurt of progress above them.

The pattern Max caught on to can be seen in the experiences of climbers of all grades. Experience shows that improvement progresses best when the difficulty of the routes you have done forms a stable pyramid. By this we mean that the numbers of routes you have done of each particular grade roughly doubles with each easier letter grade as you descend from the top of your pyramid. For a climber whose hardest route is 5.12b, a stable pyramid would look something like the below figure.

If your pyramid is wider and flatter than this, chances are you're solid in your grades. You have a good base on which to stack harder routes, and you'd probably progress faster by trying more difficult climbs and heightening your pyramid. A wide, flat pyramid indicates potential for a higher peak.

If your pyramid is taller and skinnier than this one, it's likely you'll have a harder time pushing your top grade any higher until you've broadened your base. When progression pyramids get tall and thin, your efforts can be easily toppled by injury, frustration, or simple failure.

Breaking into new grades can be incred-

Hardest Route Pyramid								Number of Routes Climbed
			12b					One 5.12b
		12a		12a				Two 5.12a's
	11d		11d		11d		11d	Four 5.11d's
11c	11c	11c	11c	11c	11c	11c	11c	Eight 5.11c's

A sample progression pyramid for a beginning 5.12 climber.

route combines all the elements that can make up 11d difficulty. Until you have a base of experience in a particular grade, trying harder routes inevitably produces more frustration than success.

The concept of the progression pyramid can help to explain many seemingly unpredictable aspects of climbing development. It explains, for instance, why the exciting breakthroughs to newer grades are often followed by unglorious phases of building onto the base and filling in the gaps in your pyramid. Although it suggests there's no shortcut to the top, it provides a model for what it takes to build your pyramid as high as you want it to be.

The progression pyramid doesn't have to be the directing principle for every route you do. When you're far from your personal limitations, your training may safely contradict its principles. But if you reach a frustrating impasse in your climbing, in the form of plateaus, regression, or injuries, consider the progression pyramid. This simple model can provide helpful direction for what to do next in your climbing.

COMPETITION TACTICS

In daily cragging, success and failure hang in the balance, and great efforts, both physical and psychological, are required to tip the scales in your favor. But the rewards and penalties for success and failure are personal and individually defined. There's only a limited amount of external pressure to do well.

Competitions up the ante of sport climbing by raising the potential for loss

ibly motivating. That's why it's sometimes worthwhile to push higher, even if you've only done a couple routes in the underlying grade. But aiming higher than your ability and experience can support is demotivating.

The hardest routes you do, whether in the redpoint or on-sight category, are built upon the experiences and successes of other routes you've done. Your performance on new routes is inseparably related to past climbs. For example, climbing your first 5.11d doesn't make you an 11d climber ready to break into 5.12a, for no single

when you perform below your ability and increasing the potential for reward when you perform well. As a result, the experience of climbing in competitions can feel like dangerous soloing or climbing runout routes where one constantly battles the restrictive inhibition that comes from the belief that one *must* climb well.

The fact that these pressures arrive in our consciousness only through our own perceptions and choices is the fundamental intrigue of competition. For at their root, these pressures are illusory. They exist only in our minds. Yet few have the mental strength to keep from buckling, to one degree or another, under their powerful influence.

The Battle against Threat

Competition makes a risk sport out of sport climbing, where ego is the object of risk. Many climbers legitimately dislike the challenge competitions offer. But those who shun them for the reason that competition is contrary to the spirit of climbing fail to understand the nature of the challenge competitions offer.

Climbers don't battle each other in competition. The presence of other competitors is only necessary to make participants create a climate of threat in their own minds. As we've seen in the Psychological Aspects sections, threat is one of the most potent performance-crippling factors. Through the threat to ego that competitions apply, the already powerful psychological component of climbing is magnified to dizzying levels. A competitor's real battle occurs within himself as he fights the tendency to botch his own performance through his encounter with a perceived threat.

There are a number of tactics that can help you confront this personal encounter head-on. But realize that these tactics are not the essence of competition. They arc merely tools to help you overcome the obstacles to meeting the real challenges of competition directly.

Warming Up

Its amazing how climbers who routinely warm up at the crag will fail to do so in a competition they take seriously. Remember, a warm-up does more than just raise your body temperature to its optimum for physical output. It also reacquaints you with the neural patterns for climbing movement, many of which may have gone unused during preceding rest days.

As a result, though you may feel warm after fifteen or twenty minutes, it takes time for a real warm-up to set in. Rather than find yourself "baked Alaska" halfway up a competition route—physically warmed up but not yet in the groove of climbing—take the time for a warm-up that soaks into the deep levels of coordination and technique. Because eccentric muscle contractions best stimulate maximum recruitment, climb both up *and* down as part of your warm-up to achieve maximum strength.

Choosing Performance-specific Goals

People enter competitions for different reasons. Some want to compare their abilities with the "hotshots," some want to burn off their rivals, others hope to win. But everyone enters competitions with a goal, whether he chooses that goal consciously or not.

Goals focus our attention. By targeting motivation, goals define what we're aware of and what we ignore. As a result, they also reduce our awareness of factors unrelated to the goal. Because goals determine where we aim our attention, it's important to choose them carefully. Not all goals further our aims; some goals can actually inhibit their own fulfillment. Goals benefit your climbing objectives only if

extra attention on the goal's focus helps you climb. They serve you only if they are specific to your performance.

Many think that the best way to do well in a competition is to choose a goal that has to do with an objective standard. "I want to place in the top half." "I want to place in the top three." "I want to flash the quarter-final and semi-final routes." "I want to win!" After all, staying acutely aware of your position and rank is critical in many types of competitions. If you're on the last mile of a bike race with three competitors ahead of you and your aim is to be in the top three yourself, your goal provides a direct focus for what you have to do. If your target position is within reach, your goal can help you handle the pain of getting there.

But such goals can't provide this focus in climbing. In an on-sight competition, you don't know how high the competitors before or after you climb. You don't know if you have to flash the route to qualify or if the course setter intended for no one to flash the route. These goals are not specific to your climbing performance.

Nonspecific climbing goals provide no focus for what you have to do to achieve them. They offer no direction while you're climbing. By focusing your mind on factors unrelated to your performance, nonspecific goals take your mind off things that might benefit from your attention.

Performance-specific goals further your abilities by focusing your mind on specific needs you have in your climbing. Since everyone has different needs, no one goal or mind-set guarantees success. Successful goals help you combat your particular weaknesses on the terrain before you.

For example, a goal of "keep breathing" can help you stay relaxed and take your mind off factors that might overarouse you in the competitive setting. Technical goals like "remember to twist your lock-offs" or "use your outside edges" can make techniques in which you lack fluency more available for your use. Awareness of these goals helps you see sequence options that wouldn't otherwise come naturally to you.

If you are aware of your greatest weaknesses in different types of climbing, or the weaknesses that crop up for you under pressure, you can formulate performance-specific goals that will help you minimize them. Follow the guidelines for goal setting we outlined in chapter 6 to maximize the effectiveness of your goals.

Finally, don't overload you mind with goals. Performance-specific goals can help you focus on one or two things that don't come naturally to you. But trying to target more than two or three issues isn't practical in a competition setting.

Training for Exact Conditions

When the Cold War was at its peak, Soviet athletes were regularly greeted by boos from Western spectators at international competitions, and their athletes were negatively affected. Rather than post formal complaints or try to cheer up the athletes, their coaches' response was to bring mock crowds into their training areas before competitions to boo at the athletes during practice. Once the gymnasts could do their routines flawlessly to the backdrop of jeers and boos, they had no more trouble with the heckling in competitions. They also became the world's best performing gymnasts.

The advantage of training for the exact conditions you'll encounter in a competition cannot be overemphasized. Your mind and body adapt to the conditions they're exposed to most often. Imagine a competition involving five routes in successive ten-minute periods. If you always have long rests after climbing a route, you won't be as prepared as if you simulated the same format in your training prior to the competition.

Preparing for the Worst

Many athletes exaggerate their training for exact conditions by preparing for the worst they might encounter. Volleyball players train with a higher net and lowered floor to force them to jump higher before a competition. Climbers train in the hot sun to prepare for a stifling competition hall.

Preparing for the worst by exaggerating it in training helps competitors accept the lack of control they have over many of the

factors that surround competition. Once in the competition itself, these unpleasant factors no longer ruffle them and distract their focus.

Bitter competitors sometimes dismiss top performances of their rivals at competitions, saying "They got lucky." But luck is rarely the whimsical bestower of fortune that this attitude assumes.

There's a saying that luck is at the crossroads of preparation and opportunity. If this is true, anyone can seek out luck by being prepared and putting herself in situations that offer opportunity. Without hard work, there are no miracles.

REFERENCES

GENERAL LITERATURE:

Adams, R. *Konditionstraining im Sportklettern.* Deutscher Alpenverein e. V. München, 1990.

Burtscher, M., and W. Nachbauer. *Motorische Leistungsfähigkeit und Gesundheitszustand von Sportkletterern.* OeAV. Innsbruck, 1989.

Deweze, S., and M. LeMenestrel. *Escalade libre.* Paris, 1987.

Godoffe, J. *Le joueur de Bloc.* Paris, 1989.

Grosser, M., P. Brüggemann, and F. Zintl. *Leistungssteuerung in Training und Wettkampf.* München, 1986.

Güllich, W. *Sportklettern heute.* Müchen, 1986.

Guyton, A.C. *Human Physiology and Mechanisms of Disease* (fourth ed.). Philadelphia: Saunders, 1987.

Harre, D. *Trainingslehre.* 10.Aufl. Berlin, 1986.

Hollmann, W., and T. Hettinger. *Sportmedizin—Arbeits und Trainingsgrundlagen.* 3.Aufl., Stuttgart, 1991.

Matwejew, L.P. *Grundlagen des sportlichen Trainings.* Berlin, 1981.

Neumann, U. *Erstellen eines Anforderungsprofils des Wettbewerbskletterns.* Diplomarbeit, DSHS Köln, 1990.

Piratinskij, A.E. *Podgotowka Skalolasa.* Moscow, 1987.

Selye, H. *The Stress of Life.* New York: McGraw-Hill, 1956.

Singer, R.N., and W. Dick. *Teaching Physical Education: A Systems Approach* (second ed.). Boston: Houghton Mifflin, 1980.

Weil, A. *Natural Health, Natural Medicine.* Boston: Houghton Mifflin Company, 1990.

PHYSICAL ASPECTS AND PHYSICAL TRAINING:

Bührle, M. "Maximalkraft-Schnellkraft-Relativkraft, Kraftkomponenten und ihre dimensionale Struktur." *Sportwissenschaft* 19. Jrg. 1989.

———. *Grundlagen des Maximal-und Schnellkrafttrainings.* Schorndorf, 1985.

Ferrand, A. "Le system de musculation a impact doux." *Magazin Montagnes* No. 94, 1987.

———. "Connais-toi, toi meme." *M. M.* No. 86, 1986.

Komi, P.V., ed. *Strength and Power in Sports.* Boston: Blackwell, 1992.

McMahon, T.A. *Muscles, Reflexes, and Locomotion.* Princeton: Princeton University Press, 1984.

Radlinger, L. *Lokale Kraftausdauer.* Theoretische und empirische Untersuchungen leistungsbestimmender Parameter. Dissertation, DSHS Köln, 1987.

Schmidt, R.F., ed. *Strength and Power in Sport.* Boston: Blackwell, 1992.

Sherrer, F. "L'entrainement physique en escalade." *Vertical* #12, Grenoble, 1987.

Sölveborn, S.A. *Das Buch vom Stretching.* Mosaik Verlag, München, 1983.

Tribout, J.B. "Les Travaux d'Hercule." *Bloc et Falaise* #1, 1986.

————. "L'escalade cocoone." *Vertical Special* #1, Grenoble, 1990.

PSYCHOLOGY AND PSYCHOTRAINING:

Bernstein, D.A., and T.D. Borkovec. *Progressive Relaxation Training.* Champaign, IL: Research Press Company, 1973.

Folkins, C.H., et al. "Desensitization and the experimental reduction of threat." *Journal of Abnormal Psychology* 73: 100–113.

Godoffe, J. "La Concentration . . . Qu'est-ce que c'est?" *Vertical* #7, Grenoble, 1986

Landers, D.M. "Motivation and performance: The role of arousal and attentional factors." In *Sport Psychology: An Analysis of Athletes' Behavior,* W.F. Straub, ed. New York, 1978.

Lawther, J.D. *Sport Psychology.* Englewood Cliffs, NJ: Prentice-Hall, 1972.

Lindsay, P.H., and D.A. Norman. *Human Information Processing—An Introduction to Psychology* (second ed.). New York: Academic Press, 1977.

Loftus, G.R., and E.F. Loftus: *Human Memory —The Processing of Information.* Hillsdale, NJ: Lawrence Erlbaum Associates, 1976.

Herrigel, E. *Zen in the Art of Archery.* New York: Pantheon Books, 1953.

COORDINATION AND TECHNIQUE TRAINING:

Brooks, V.B. *The Neural Basis of Motor Control.* New York: Oxford University Press, 1986.

Dickinson, J. *Proprioceptive Control of Human Movement.* London: Lepus Books, 1974.

Drowatzky, J.N. *Motor Learning, Principles and Practices.* Minneapolis: Burgess Publishing Company, 1975.

Evarts, E.V., S.P. Wise, and D. Bousfield, eds. *The Motor System in Neurobiology.* New York: Elsevier, 1985.

Gowitzke, B.A. *Scientific Bases of Human Movement.* Baltimore: Williams & Wilkins, 1988.

Grosser, M., and A. Neumaier. *Techniktraining.* München, 1982.

Kaas, J.H. "Plasticity of sensory and motor maps in adult mammals." *Annual Review of Neuroscience* 14, 137–167.

Matthews, P.B.C. "Where does Sherrington's muscular sense originate? Muscles, joints, corollary discharges?" *Annual Review of Neuroscience* 5, 198–218.

Meinel, K., and G. Schnabel. *Bewegungslehre—Sportmotorik.* 8.Aufl., Berlin 1987.

Roth, K. *Strukturanalyse Koordinativer Fähigkeiten.* Bad Hamburg, 1982.

Rothwell, J.C. *Control of Human Voluntary Movement.* Rockville, MD: Aspen Publications, 1987.

Schmidt, R.A. *Motor Control and Learning—A Behavioral Emphasis.* Champaign, IL: Human Kinetics Publishers, 1982.

Singer, R.N. *Motor Learning and Human Performance* (second ed.). New York: MacMillan Publishing Company, 1975.

Somjen, G. *Neurophysiology: The Essentials.* Baltimore: Williams & Wilkins, 1983.

Stein, J.F. "The control of movement." In *Functions of the Brain,* C.W. Coen, ed. Oxford: Clarendon Press, 1985.

STAYING HEALTHY:

Bollen, S.R., and C.K. Gunson. "Hand injuries in competition climbers." *British Journal of Sports Medicine,* vol. 24 #1, 1990.

Maitland, M. "Injuries associated with rock climbing." *JOSPT,* vol. 16 #2, 1992.

Weil, A. *Health and Healing.* Boston: Houghton Mifflin Company, 1988.

the ACCESS FUND

...preserving America's diverse climbing resources.

Continued freedom to climb depends on all of us. You can help keep your favorite crags open to climbing.

Conservation equals Access... a few easy habits make the difference. Keep climbing areas litter-free. Dispose of human waste properly. Stay on established trails whenever possible. Respect local regulations, or work to change them legally, through the Access Fund.

Another good habit: support the Access Fund. Your donation is tax-deductible, and will be used to build trails, buy land, finance scientific studies and for other crucial projects that help preserve access.

The Access Fund is working to keep you climbing.
Send your donation today to:

The Access Fund • PO Box 17010 • Boulder, CO 80308

"There's not a climber who won't be touched by some element of *Performance Rock Climbing.*"

— World Cup winner Robyn Erbesfield

Rock Climbing